The Goat Foot God

Diotima

BIBLIOTHECA ALEXANDRINA

Printed by CreateSpace in the United States of America

Dedication

To Liutas – who kindly and patiently dealt with conversations about ComPanion for far too long....

To the Black Rock.... who offered support and challenge...

To he who may be known as Chrysostom – he will understand why...

To the Silent Shadows, wherein I hide and am held...

To my family, who are all.... And the kookaburra who brings joy and beauty

To those who read and who never will read this book...

And to the Principal Character.

Table of Contents

Introduction

Pan....

This book is not about "what we know about Pan."

If it were to be such, it would need to include work from everyone who has thought about, read about, encountered, fulminated against, or shouted about Pan, as well as all artwork about him. Clearly, this is neither possible nor useful – one man's Pan, after all, is another man's goat.

So what is this book about?

Simply: Pan, as written about, as worshipped, as interacted with, and as depicted in paint, stone and paper. (Oh, and pixels, what with the rise of internet technology.) I make no claim to be exhaustive in this endeavour, nor do I claim to read into works of art or literature, to divine their "real" meaning. My work here is slanted toward the ancient rather than the modern. And I hope that the reader will come out with a decidedly lopsided view of the great god Pan.

Why lopsided?

Because Pan is, above all things, entirely his own, and fits not into our moulds of balance or complacency.

His study, however, is a great deal of fun.

I intend this study to be slightly less chaotic than the god who is its subject – at least somewhat.

I shall begin – as the song impels us to do – "at the very beginning" – or at least as far back as one can go in the literature (which is, if we take a Greek at his word, rather far indeed). In fact, the ideas of the ancients will form the bulk of this work, as they provide the foundation of what follows.

Yet while the Greek lore about Pan is vital to any study of him, it's not the be all and end all – among all the epithets given to him throughout time, I am unaware of *anyone* calling him "static" or implying that he could be such a thing. He is movement (Plato), the running of the herd, the rutting of the ram – not some of these, but all, and more – and as such, he defies categorisations. Wisely, for the most part the Greeks avoided trying to put him in categories at all.[1]

The written word conjures images – and there are more than enough images of Pan and his kin to be going on with, from the ancient world.

Our fascination with Pan didn't end with the Golden age of Greece, nor with the fall of Rome. Whether or not the goat-gods depicted by so many witch finders have anything to do with Pan, I cannot say, but certainly the overt namings of the god reappear with the Romantics and remain with us – from Burne-Jones to Machen (1894), from encounters with small, fluffy animals (Grahame 1917) to epic tales of beets (Robbins 2001).

As I have said, this depiction of the Great God will not be complete and it will be decidedly idiosyncratic. However, I hope it will also be of use.

A note about sources, etc.

While not technically an academic work, this book will follow general academic conventions, at least to some extent, in that sources for ideas, dates, etc. will be cited whenever possible.

Citations are in the format known as "Harvard," as this seems the least intrusive way of doing things – author and date (for modern works) are cited in the text, while full bibliographic information will be found in the eponymous appendix.

Ancient texts will not generally have a date accompanying the citation, although obviously dates of editions will be given in the references. There is something profoundly disturbing about seeing "Euripides, 2001" in a line of text.

Footnotes, therefore, are not required as a means of citation or referencing. They are, however, used freely as a means of expanding on the text, giving further information which might otherwise interrupt the

---

[1] If one takes Keller's word for it, indeed, trying to categorise much about early Greek society at all is an exercise in futility (Keller 1910).

flow of the narrative, or indeed, simply for making the author's point of view on various issues rather more clear. It is the prerogative of authors to do this sort of thing; at least I generally have the decency to be clear about what I am doing in such cases.

Mind set

I have said above that this will not be – that there can never be – a definitive text on Pan.

This would be the case even if an author were to limit herself to the ancient views of and dealings with the goat foot god. And this would be due to no lack in the author, but rather to a change in emphasis, a change in culture – a sea change in that which we find important[2].

Before continuing with this chapter, it is important that this change is made clear – even if it may be impossible for us today to completely understand it. To put it simply: we don't think in quite the same way our ancestors did. To put it another way: we're far more limited and I have a suspicion that an ancient Athenian or Roman, plonked down in a pub in the middle of London or a bar in New York, would quickly be saddened by the single-mindedness and lack of breadth encountered. (Though how they would feel about the music is another matter entirely...)

The best explanation of this change I've seen is in the introduction to *The Battle for God*, by Karen Armstrong (2000). I would highly recommend reading the original, but for the moment (assuming it's not always possible to wander off to find a particular book) I will summarise the point she makes about the difference between what she calls "logos" and "mythos."

We are, she maintains, solidly people of logos – we want the rational, the sensible, the "true," and we are sure that this is the way things should be, when we stop to consider it at all. Think for a moment about our view of history. Historians know that it is not a de facto record, but rather what was recorded, what survived and is almost always slanted in one way or another (Carr 1961), but for the rest of us,

---

[2] Even such a metaphor relates, for Pan is reckoned to have connections to the sea, at least by some ancient authors ...

history is seen as (and to be fair, presented as) "the truth" of what happened in the past.

We discount that which we do not see as "real" as being of less importance. We wish for proof of the most mundane things, and assume that such proof will be forthcoming for the most esoteric, as well (consider all the discussions in print, on websites, on fora, etc. about whether or not magick "works" and who can prove it does).

A very good example of this may be found in the introduction to the excellent *Dictionary of Ancient History* put out by Penguin (Speake 1994). Speaking of the companion volume which deals with mythology, Speake says, "The publisher helpfully distinguishes the two books by describing that one as being concerned with the 'pretend' people of antiquity while ours is concerned with the 'real' people" (ix)."[3]

This is, I believe, a very good example of the difference between logos and mythos – and indeed, of the arrogance of logos itself. Only what is provable, only what is acknowledged as "true" by the academy, is considered real, no matter what those involved in the original belief may have thought.

But even here, it is impossible for the author to make his case stand without some prevarication, for he continues, "We have, however, been permitted to include a few 'pretend' people in this volume: it would, for example, be absurd to try to tell the story of Greek medicine without reference to Asclepius or the Delphic oracle without Apollo..."

Logos is that mind set, that point of view which seeks logic, rationality, proof, above all. Mythos is that mind set that allows, indulges in ambiguity, the unseen, the non-rational. For a people living in the midst of mythos, many of our modern[4] questions make no sense.

---

[3] It would be interesting to compare this to volumes dealing with other religious systems: in a work on the history of Christianity, are there those who, lacking historical "proof" of their existence, would be defined as "pretend"? Or are only the deities not acknowledged by the majority of a society so labelled?

[4] Some may argue that our questions are actually post-modern, due to the age in which we live. I suspect, however, that the impacts of post-modernity will take far more than a few generations to filter through to most ordinary people; they certainly have yet to affect things such as the media, the school curricula, etc.

As Armstrong points out, asking if the biblical story of creation actually took place over seven days would make little or no sense to those who first told it – that wasn't the point they were trying to make. Such questions may be akin, I suspect, to concentrating on the stitching in one area of embroidery and missing the story that the Bayeux tapestry is trying to tell us... To put it another way, myths are never static, they do not form a museum, but rather are a vibrant (if we let them be so) means of communication (Borgeaud 1988).

The point of this excursus is to set the stage for what follows. The logos-oriented mind will find the parts of this book dealing with the ancient world confusing, frustrating and "lacking in coherence."

That's because they are.

But then, they were never meant to be anything other – because they were meant to reflect, as accurately and holistically as possible, ancient practice and belief (Garland 1994). I refuse to assemble the disparate (sometimes *very* disparate) elements dealing with Pan and enforce some sort of alien order upon them.

The logos-oriented mind will seek for "the" way the ancient Greeks related to Pan, for "the" rituals to appease/please him, for "the" title he was given, for "the" myth or myths which "best" explain him. Such a mind will be disappointed. The situation is similar to that of western students when confronted with ancient Egyptian belief and its numerous creation stories. Over and over again, students ask, "yes, but which one did they *believe*?" because of course (they assume) there must have been only one. The mythos-related mind, on the other hand, accepts both/all of the stories and revels in the differences and connections between them, without the need to assign superiority to one or the other[6]. They are all accepted as being of worth *for the value they were meant to have*. One may teach that humans are intimately connected to the rest of the world, another that life is transitory, another something different....

---

[6] One is reminded of the rabbi on a radio programme who, when asked if the story of Adam and Eve was literally true, said, "Oh, no – it's *much* more important than that!"

"Greece…" even "Ancient Greece…"

These words bring a variety of images to our minds – vases in red and black, men and women in draped clothes, Trojan horses and golden face masks… for those of us of a certain age, images of "the wine dark sea."

It has been said that Greece exists for us more as an "inscape" than an "outscape" – that is, we are so sure what it was like, we have convinced ourselves what it was like that we don't really need the reality and indeed, do not want to know about it. We proclaim ourselves the proud inheritors of the Greek ideals of democracy and fair play, of philosophy and gentility.

We might, then, be rather surprised by the reality which was far bloodier, far less fair and in no real way democratic. The "Ancient Greece" that most of us think about is actually quite a small section of what might be covered by that term – we tend to think of Classical Athens, in the fourth and third centuries BCE. In reality, people have been in Greece since at least 50,000 BCE (and quite possibly longer, but it is from this stage that artefacts become plentiful) (Barber 1998). Greece was, throughout the period in which we are interested (that is, from at least the time of the *Iliad* and *Odyssey* through to the early Christian period), a war-like, slave owning, male dominated, militaristic society, in which the ultimate authority in the family was the eldest male[7] and in which, for the middle classes, at least, the glory of woman was to be spoken of in neither praise nor blame. The concept of "democracy" never included more than about one of every ten men, and no women at all. Infanticide was a well known practice (see below), human sacrifice was not unknown.

Yet we still see Greece as a shining example of what we should be, what we might be – a function as much of the legacy of the Renaissance as of Greece itself.

---

[7] Indeed, an actual patriarchy, in the proper sense of the word.

There is no way to understand what the Greeks thought about Pan without some understanding of religion, ritual, epic and myth in Greek society. However, as delaying our discussion of Pan for long to engage in such diversions would be not only off-putting but would likely be skipped over by most readers, I will be as brief as possible (and invite the interested reader to avail herself of the works cited in the bibliography).

Myths

This is not the place for an in-depth look at what myth is, how it functions in society or societies, what value it has, or what value should be accorded to it. There are more than enough texts which will supply this information, from a *Very Short Introduction* (Segal 2004) through to far weightier tomes (Campbell 1949; Kirk 1970; Maranda 1972; Strenski 1987; Carroll 1992; Estes 1992; Eliot 1993; Grimal 1996; Campbell 2001; Larson 2001; Sykes and Kendall 2002; Diotima 2004; Price and Kearns 2004; Armstrong 2005). For our purposes, it is enough to enunciate a few clear themes.

The first is that myth does not equal untrue. As is obvious from the previous section, "myth" is a different sort of beast from "logic" and therefore the criteria by which one might judge the second do not apply to the first. What matters is not what the name of the young boy was, or where he was from or how old he was, but rather that his incessant cry of "wolf, wolf!" annoyed those around him to the extent that they ignored the normal social order and did not, as adults, rush to the defence of a child. The moral (that unwarranted demands are, in the long run, destructive) requires merely enough internal consistence to be believable, not enough to be verifiable.[8]

The second follows from this – that the value of the myth is inherent in the myth itself, and what it tells us, not in its application further afield. We will look at a good number of ancient myths about Pan which may

---

[8] Myths may also have meanings which are so obvious, we miss them: in this case, that the normal social order *is* that adults will rush to the defence and aid of children.

seem to have little relevance for us today – after all, not that many reading this book will be full, or even part time shepherds... That does not mean, however, that there is nothing we can learn from them.

Gods[9]

It can be very difficult for the Western mind, which is not only deeply steeped in logos and logic but has probably also been heavily influenced by religions of the book, to understand (in Heinlein's word, to "grok") the ancient view of deity, or the non-Abrahamic view of deity, if you will.

We may understand that the concept of monotheism (there is only one God) did not generally obtain in the ancient world, and we may know various stories and myths. But there is more to understanding ancient deities than this – there is a fairly fundamental change of mind set needed.

To put it simply, in the Abrahamic religions (Judaism, Christianity, Islam), deity is fundamentally concerned with humanity and generally has humanity's best interests at heart. Prayers are answered, the just are rewarded, there is a standard to be upheld, and a book to judge that standard by.

The Greeks would not have understood this concept of deity, and indeed, did not. (Note I mean ordinary Greeks, not the philosophers, who were always rather a breed apart, what with all that wandering about wet and mumbling, the bean-based diets and so on). Aside from some of the mystery cults, there was no general sense that the gods would reward the just – rather, they tended to choose their favourites on very different grounds (Garland 1994). Their interactions with humans were capricious at best – after all, it's arguable that the Trojan war was the result of one god feeling slighted and inciting others to riot in response. In fact, this lack of consistency led to some of the

---

[9] Note that "god" here is being used as a generic. In the interests of fair play, "goddess" will be used as an equally inclusive term. The male may embrace the female, but in this century of the fruit bat, the female is quite likely to embrace back... (Diotima 2005)

philosophical calls for an end to mythmaking and retelling: after all, one can hardly argue that some of the gods were in any way good role models for a stable society![10]

But then, they were never meant to be such – which is where the mind steeped in the religions of the book may come a little unstuck. Try to remember, however, that the Greek gods were answerable only to themselves, rather than to any sort of systematic theology which sought to make one proposition (such as "God is good") align with any other (such as "God will judge the righteous"). The closest the Greek myths might come to such a theology would be a series of quite possibly contradictory statements which boiled down to: "Don't annoy them."[11]

Greek Religion

There are many fine texts available about Greek religion, and I have no intention (and no need) to reproduce their bulk here. However, once again the contemporary reader must understand certain basic points if she is to comprehend anything of the cult[12] (what there was of it – and why or why not the presence of such a cult is important) of the goat foot god among the ancients.

---

[10] In Garland's phrase, "The primary reason why the gods could not be the upholders of the moral order is that they simply were not qualified. Their track record was lousy." (Garland 1994, 4) He goes on to speak of the various vices indulged in by the Greek deities. While it might be very interesting to engage in this debate – who sets the moral code, is it possible for gods to transgress that code (and so be vicious), does that moral code apply to the gods, etc. – this is not the place for such discussion. The general point is well made, however: the gods may have been the guardians of specific ideals, but not of virtue (or lack-of-sin, if you will), overall.

[11] "...the Greeks did not worship their gods because they upheld justice or were supremely good beings They worshipped them because they were powerful and because it could be extremely dangerous not to worship them." (Garland 1994, p. 6)

[12] "Cult" here is being used in its specific meaning of, "a series of practices, dedicated practices aligned to a specific set of beliefs (religion)." It is in this sense that one may speak of the cult of Demeter or the Virgin Mary, rather than the cult of whatever set of raving loonies has most recently hit the headlines.

And the first is that "religion" as we know it, would quite possibly be very difficult for an ancient Greek to understand – certainly explaining the idea to her would be difficult, as there is no word for what we mean by "religion," even in the word-rich language that is classical Greek (Garland 1994; Faraone 2004). This doesn't mean that they did not *have* a religion – though it would be far more accurate to say that they practiced religion, rather than had it. It does mean, however, that the grouping of ideas, actions and emotions which we designate by the name "religion" is a grouping that they did not, in fact, make.

Many modern Pagans, (practitioners of Hellenismos among them) walk an uneasy line between their own, avowed declarations of eclecticism, and not being tied to any one text, and an almost fanatical desire to verify their own beliefs and practices by recourse to historical documents – for indeed, whatever our own beliefs, we are a *society* of the book[13].

Greek society and religion certainly had books and texts: what it did not have was **a** text – a Bible or Koran – that had the status of "a holy book." Nor did it have a caste of people (men, generally…) set apart from the common herd to act as priests. Not that there were not those who performed priestly functions – of course there were. But generally not to the exclusion of other deities and almost always, only to fulfil a role in ritual, rather than as a life choice, or a teaching role (Burkert 1985).

Therefore, I am leaving the detailed discussions of provenance of documents, etc. to the experts – since none of them must be treated as sacrosanct, none need be given that much in depth discussion. Nor need we consider whether or not any mediator is needed for knowledge: the Greeks simply didn't work in that way, where their deities were concerned, and I see no need to start doing so now.

---

[13] And I am no exception – look at the constant references I provide to… books.

Arcadia

A word about Arcadia is perhaps in order at this point...

Arcadia was the place of "those who preceded the moon," according to the ancients; Aristotle credits the Arcadians with having ousted the resident barbarians and settled the place (Constitution on Tegea, cited in Borgeaud 1988); Ovid holds that they are "older than Jupiter and the moon" (Fasti), which is a remarkable pedigree, considering the value put on genealogies and provenance by ancient society. It's possible that Aristotle's comment is not about "going into battle before moonrise" but rather to "before the moon was around to rise in the first place" (Borgeaud 1988). Living before the moon might have been a bit tricky, but apparently one could subsist on acorns, if not much else (Apollonius Rhodius).[14]

We tend to think of "Arcadia" as a blissful place –almost the place of the happy, noble savage. In this, we follow the Roman tradition, such as that Virgil gives in relation to the founding of Rome, which sees Arcadia as an idyllic landscape. The Greeks, however, knew better – any place which survives on goat herding and hunting is going to be far from idyllic and indeed, far from an easy place to earn (or make) a crust; it was, rather, "a barren and forbidding land inhabited by rude, almost wild primitives, a place where music primarily has the function of softening manners" (Borgeaud 1988, 6). Or, as the same author puts it in another place, "Arcadia is primitive but strong (the warriors eat acorns) and its integrity cannot be lightly challenged" (pg. 10). This view is upheld by Pausanias, who records that Pelasgus, the first king of Arcadia, invented the idea of living in huts, of making coats of sheepskin, and moved people away from eating poisonous grasses and roots, and to the eating of the ubiquitous acorns (Pausanias, 8.1.4 - 5). So while not as advanced as those who till the soil (which is going to be very difficult to do in Arcadia, to be fair), the area is more advanced that those who

---

[14] In one of those coincidences which probably mean nothing but are none the less pleasing, the Arcadians in theory descend from Dryops – a name which means "oaken faced" –which might well be a very good epithet for those who are constantly to be seen eating acorns...

live rough, without a centre to their wanderings with the herds, and who eat whatever comes to hand, rather than planning ahead and harvesting when necessary.

That grain, and living on grain rather than acorns, eventually arrives in Arcadia, is without doubt – for Triptolemus[15] shares the secret of grain with Arcadians, and civilization as the Greeks recognise it begins with the second generation of Arcadian rulers (Borgeaud 1988).

All in all, a fitting place for the origin of Pan and his cult – a place which is bound to be close to his heart, for he shares so many of its (perceived) characteristics.

A note about status...

There are those who have recourse to the ancient texts about the gods as though to a sacred text, set in stone. If we are told by the ancients that Pan is always seen as half god/half goat (and we are told no such thing), then it is impossible, if not heretical, to suppose that he can be seen or thought of in any other way.

In other words, the ancient works are accorded an untouchable status, as though they were somehow the final word on the gods, and any experience of those gods today must be made to fit in with the ancient texts.

Yet, when you come right down to it, what are those texts, in actuality?

They are the records of people's thoughts, beliefs and experiences.

What gives those experiences, those thoughts, priority over our own? While I have no issue with the concept of respecting one's elders (and indeed, my ever-advancing age means it's in my interest to promote such ideals), I see no reason that someone else's experience should have priority over mine, simply because that experience occurred thousands of years ago and is recorded in books deemed to be "classics."

---

[15] A link with the myths/rituals of Eleuisis? There is no way to know, but the possibility is tantalising...

Further, does not insistence on the ancient texts hem in the gods themselves[16]? In a previous section, I pointed out a rather significant change that our own minds have gone through in the last few thousand years: are we to assume that deity does not change? Who am I to tell the goat foot god that he *must* always be found in fields, rather than in the city? (I know too much of the lore to say any such thing, anyway, but you see the point.)

There is, of course, a sense of "what this god or that would do" that originates with whatever texts are oldest about that particular deity, and then builds up. Saying that Pan can be found in the city would not startle me at all. Saying, however, that he had taken a job which required him to not only wear a suit but be active every day, all day, *would* startle me, simply because it goes against so much of what others have known/experienced about him.

That would not, however, give me the right to tell you that you were wrong, if you felt that this was your experience of Pan...

The point here is that privileging the experiences of the ancients over those of our own day is the worst kind of reverse snobbery. Is it important to know what the Athenians thought of Pan? Clearly, I think so, or I'd not finish writing this book. Do I think their views have priority over anyone else's? No – experience is experience, whether it's 350 BC or 2008 AD.

---

[16] One might also consider the effect of such a belief on the deity – in the style of the effect on those within the pages of Pratchett's *Small Gods* (Pratchett 1992).

The origins of the Goat Foot God

> The rustic god Pan chanced to be sitting at that moment on the brow of the stream ... Close by the bank nanny-goats were sporting as they grazed and cropped the river-foliage here and there. The goat-shaped god ... said: 'I am a rustic herdsman."
> (Apuleius 1999)

Here – at least if we take the word of Apuleius – we have the words of Pan himself about what and who he is – a rustic herdsman.

The problem of taking this statement at face value, however, immediately presents itself. Apuleius, in common with most of the rest of the sources cited here, was not generally in the habit of recording the words of rustic herdsmen for posterity – why should he do so? Yet these words, and many others like them, *were* recorded and are still there for us to read, peruse and ponder.

The earliest literary information we have about Pan is probably from the Homeric Hymn to him (Merivale 1969), number 19 of that grouping, if one is counting. The Hymns almost certainly weren't written by Homer; rather, they are in his style, and so fit within the corpus of work which is given the general title. Whoever wrote them, (and it is to Thucydides that we owe the attribution to Homer, so we can at least blame him), the Hymns form one of the basic building blocks of western literature (Richardson 2003).

The Hymns are a series of songs – four are long and complex (to Aphrodite, Apollo, Demeter and Hermes), and were probably created (if not written down – therein lies an entirely different argument (Notopoulos 1962; Nagy 1992)) within a hundred years either way of 500 BCE. It's thought that the other, shorter poems (29 in all, including that to Pan) are later (Burkert 1985). Although scholars are still not entirely agreed about their function, it would seem that the longer Hymns, at least, were more about imparting and preserving myth than about liturgy or formal worship (Speake 1994).

Of course, the Hymns may well have been written down long after they were composed, like so much other oral poetry and epic. Our society seems to have little time for learning by memorisation (Diotima 2006), but we may well be unusual in that regard – simply because something was written down does not mean it was no longer recited or sung (Notopoulos 1962). (And the proliferation of Internet sites offering lyrics to popular songs does not in any way detract from the singing of those songs, in our own time.)

While we cannot and should not take the Hymns as some kind of liturgical primer, giving us a clear view of Greek religious practice, it does seem clear that the songs and chants involved performed some function in Greek society (Nagy 1992) (otherwise, why would they have been so carefully preserved?).[17] It may be that they were aetiological, in that they told the story of the origin of certain things and practices – such as the lyre and the use of a 12 part sacrifice (Richardson 2003). But it also seems possible – probable? – that some of the Hymns, notably those to Dionysus, Hestia and Hermes – and, most importantly for our purposes, that to Pan – may well have been designed for particular religious festivals.

While I've said above that there were no set texts in Greek religion, it's worth pointing out that some texts had more status than others, being referred to time and time again – the Hymns, and other works attributed to Homer and Hesiod among them (Burkert 1985). They did not have the authority attributed to the Bible nor yet that given to the Koran, but they were seen, if you like, as the basis on which all else was built. (This makes some of their omissions even more interesting, as we shall see.)

And, while the Greeks really had no equivalent to a lectionary or a book of common prayer, no primer of "how to invoke," there were certain recognised ways of going about things: if you wanted something, you followed a fairly set pattern. You made sure you got the right god listening to you (after all, the chthonic Apollo is a very

---

[17] For discussions of this phenomenon, generally called "functionalism," please refer to any reasonable sociology text book. In very condensed form, the idea is that things survive in society – any given society – as long as they fulfil a function. The reader is invited to muse, then, on the proliferation of "reality" TV – and fear.

different entity, or differently interested entity, at least, from the Apollo of the lyre), by giving the deity the full titles you want to invoke, and you reminded them of their favoured places, as well as their past deeds. (Think of asking a boss for a raise – it might well be better to tell the boss how good they are and how much you have learned from them, at the outset, than to say that you really need to pay off that loan...) Having got the god's attention (the right kind of attention from the right god), *then* you made your request, generally in connection with a sacrifice. As above, the gods weren't all that interested in humans per se: asking for something usually required that you make it worth the god's while (Garland 1994). One of the functions of the Hymns, then, was to act as a primer for such rituals: they told you where the god was born, or what she was known for, and gave you the wherewithal to contact them in as safe a manner as possible.

The Hymns tell us something about how people and gods related to each other. At times the relation is just that and the union of deity and human leads to the birth of a rather exceptional person; but more generally, the interchange is one of worship and sacrifice on our part and (often rather capricious) favour on theirs (Richardson 2003). And, in the case of Hymn 19, they tell us a bit about how the gods deal with each other as well....

The Homeric Hymn to Pan

While it's probable that this is one of the later Hymns in the collection, scholars are no more agreed on the dating than on any other aspect of the Hymns (starting with Allen 1897, and going on from there); but it seems doubtful that it is among the older Hymns; there is a bit of a silence in general Greek literature about the goat foot god in the earliest times.

Whatever its age, however, the Hymn provides a very useful structure for an examination of the ancient ideas of Pan.

That is not to say that it is the *best* ancient description of Pan, or the most accurate, or indeed the most representative – as we shall see, there are some surprising inclusions and some even more surprising omissions in the Hymn. However, it still provides a useful framework.[18]

A caveat, however: there is always a danger in deconstructing any ritual, sacred, or otherwise "different" piece of literature – that it will lose that sense of awe and wonder which *makes* it other. I would dislike this to happen to Hymn 19…

Therefore, may I ask that now, at this juncture, the reader take her/himself to Appendix 1, and reads the Hymn in its entirety? Read it in whatever way seems fitting to you – and then return to the text.

I'll wait….

Homeric Hymn to Pan – part the first

Before I begin, it is worthwhile saying that my division of Hymn 19 is entirely idiosyncratic, rather than scholarly: I make no pretence that different parts were written or constructed at different times, different locations or by different poets.[19] Rather, the divisions will be used merely to section off ideas about the god; as such, they will be uneven in length and content.

> Muse - speak to me of the loved child of Hermes with his goat's feet and his two horns, the one who loves noise, who roams about, in wooded meadows together with dancing nymphs who tread upon peaks of rock even goats leave bare - calling out "Pan" - god of shepherds - dust-parched - with dazzling hair - who has all the snowy crests and the mountain ridges and the rocky paths for his home.
>
> Here and there he roams, through dense thickets and sometimes, he is drawn to soft streams and sometimes he

---

[18] Chaoists: feel free to substitute the word "paradigm" here.

[19] According to Allen, at any rate, such an attempt is doomed to failure (Allen 1904).

wanders back over precipices of rock – climbing up to the highest peak to watch over his sheep.

(This rendition takes some liberties with the text – given in better form in the Appendix; presented in this fashion, however, it is easier to read for our purposes.)

This first section of the Hymn mentions at the outset three of the four things most people know about Pan: that he bears a physical resemblance to a goat[20]; that he is a god of the countryside (which does not mean "god of animals" – see below); and that Pan and noise go together. (The fourth – his sexual nature – doesn't really appear in the Hymn, which is in itself interesting.)

Why a goat?[21]

One answer – the simplest and perhaps most accurate – is, "because that's what Pan looks like." Simple can be simplistic, however: there was something – or somethings – about goats that not only appealed to the ancient Greeks but made sense to them in terms of the type of God they thought Pan to be.

It is tempting to say that the first likeness between Pan and goats is ubiquity – the ancient Greeks would have known all about goats, and in Arcadia, at least, they seem to have known all about Pan. Goats have been domesticated for around ten thousand years – a long pedigree of working with people. (However, anyone who knows domestic goats

---

[20] Not all the ancient authorities agreed that Pan was always a goat, however. Hyginus maintains that during the battle with Typhon, various gods changed their shapes through terror; Pan's lower half became a fish, his upper half a goat, allowing him to escape from the monster. This, according to Hyginus, explains why the constellation Capricorn has (or can have) the lower body of a fish: the constellation exists not only because the chief of the gods was nourished along with Pan, but in thanks for the panic which was cast by Pan into the Titans during their struggle against the Olympians. (Hyginus, Astronomica II.28)

[21] Almost all of the ancient sources agree that Pan is part animal – Socrates uses the term, "dual nature" (Plato; Merivale 1969). It is worth noting that even on this basic "fact," there was not agreement (see previous note) – but it must also be said that this is by far a minority view, and rarely depicted in ancient representations of Pan.

knows that "domesticated" may be a bit of a misnomer!) Goats are also extremely useful – they provide milk and hair during their lives, and meat and skin post mortem. (A parallel to one of the few – if not the only – Greek gods whose death was solemnly proclaimed?) As Stroszeck points out, it's almost impossible to overestimate the value of goats to early societies (Stroszeck 2002).

Goats are notorious for eating almost anything that comes into their path – many a child has emerged from a petting zoo without their shoelaces. For those scraping a living on rocky hillsides of Arcadia ("peaks of the rocks..."), goats are a god-send, because they need less care than many other creatures. A shepherd or goatherd[22] needs to keep an eye on the flock as a whole, but as we shall see, a nap in the afternoon is not seen as dereliction of duty – goats are fairly self-reliant.

Moreover, goats have two other, well known characteristics: the males have a rather strong scent (to be polite about it) when near does in heat, and both sexes are able to (and happy to) reproduce all year round in temperate climates. While there is little mention of Pan having a goat-like scent in ancient sources (perhaps because personal hygiene wasn't as important or possible to and for our ancestors as it is for us?), at least one author refutes the idea of Pan sharing the scent of his goats (Longus). On the other hand a modern author disagrees and endows Pan with a decidedly goat-y aroma as an essential plotline element (Robbins 2001).

The second characteristic – the randiness of the goat – is well known as a characteristic of Pan, even exemplified in the famous sculpture hidden for so long in the "secret" museum in Naples, which shows the god in happy congress with a member of the aforementioned species. It is interesting, then, that there is no real mention of this trait in the Hymn – why not?

It could be argued that the propensity for amorous encounters is implicit in the Hymn's mentions of dancing, etc., but this would be a shaky argument indeed. The fact is that the Homeric Hymn sees Pan as a

---

[22] Apologies to anyone who now must deal with an ear-worm from the Sound of Music...

hunter, a singer and dancer (and indeed, master of the dance and chorus), but not as the lecher that other tales depict – in the Hymn, he's more likely to direct the feet of a nymph than to chase her with designs on her virtue (cf. Pitys).

While it is tempting to find a pat explanation for this omission, I don't believe one exists; I've certainly never seen one in print. However, such an omission is a rather large one, and presents (to the modern mind, anyway) a vision of Pan which is at least somewhat askew from what one might expect, and thus requires some attempt at explanation... even if we acknowledge at the outset that the explanation will be incomplete and speculative.

It is possible that the writer of the Hymn assumed that everyone knew that aspect of Pan so well that it didn't need to be mentioned; this explanation has the appeal of being obvious.

It is also possible that the author of the Hymn wanted to emphasise the pastoral elements of the life of the goat foot god, rather than his sexual proclivities. What is unlikely is that the author felt that such proclivities were unbecoming a god, or were unfit for songs sung in "polite" company; our view of propriety and those of the ancient Greeks do not accord in this instance. Homes in the classical period, at least, would often have a "Herm" outside of them – think of a tall, fairly thin plank of wood, set in the ground, with a face and an erect phallus, and you've got the idea. Sculptures and artwork we might class as "erotic" might well have been on open display with no one taking much notice of it, if the remains of that civilisation are to be believed (even if we do section off those bits of pottery, etc., into "secret" musea and write books about them as a separate genre (Johns 1989)).

Perhaps, if the Hymn really was composed for a choral competition or used as a means of practice for same, it simply made sense to emphasise the music related activities in the god's life?

We shall never know – but the omission remains intriguing.

Omission must not be thought to equal ignorance, however. The earliest depictions of Pan are united on his half-goat appearance; as Merivale says, "The paradox of a being half goat and half god is the very core of his nature." (Merivale 1969, p.1)

What we do know, from the first line of the Hymn, is that Pan was loved.

It's not entirely clear from the context whether or not we are meant to take the epithet of "much loved child" as meaning that Hermes loved his son greatly (as he is clearly shown to do, further on in the poem), or that Pan is generally much loved. No other god in the Hymns is given this title, however: they are variously introduced as "strong," "beautiful," etc., but no one else is called the "loved."

And indeed, what is not to love? The picture presented of Pan in this Hymn is a light-hearted one, of a good hunter and musician – someone you would like to have around both during the day and in the celebrations that follow a successful hunt. Indeed, he is the quintessential Arcadian; as boys there were raised to music in a way unique in Greece (Polybius, 4.20). There is nothing here (yet) of panic or over amorousness. It would be possible to read too much into the phrase, "much loved," as it does not recur as a title for Pan – but it is interesting that it is given only to him.

Pan is described in this early part of the Hymn as having "dazzling hair" – an interesting epithet for someone who is also "dust-parched!" Pan's hair rarely if ever gets mentioned in other texts; depictions of him, however, generally show a good, if shaggy, head of hair; this all seems to be part of the view of Pan as a mature (at least in years) man, rather than a beardless, callow youth (he is generally seen bearded – as befits someone who is part goat, after all).

He is seen here as moving among the peaks, almost certainly those of Arcadia, of Mount Lycaeus; elsewhere, the god refers to himself as "mountain bred" (Lucian). The Arcadians were considered to be a pure Pelasgi stock, and the cult of Pan seems to be similarly pure: without the introduction of "foreign" elements; they honoured Pan equally with Zeus (Borgeaud 1988). It has been suggested that their simple, pastoral lives were the reason for their love of music (Codellas 1945); I find that difficult to reconcile with the status of music throughout society: is there or has there ever been a society that does not indulge in, and value, music?[23] At any rate, it seems that there were few, if any, ancient rituals that lacked music and/or dance (Burkert 1985).

But Pan – and his cult – were not confined to Arcadia. It would seem that the worship of Pan was widespread at least by the fifth century before the common era, if not before; again, he is not a newcomer among the gods (Borgeaud 1988). (This also means, of course, that the Hymn to Pan need not have originated in Arcadia (Allen 1904).)[24]

And these peaks, he calls his home. There is never a sense that Pan is unwelcome on Olympus – see below – but again, he is never really thought to be a long term resident there. Perhaps there is a family trait here? His grandmother, Maia, (mother of Hermes) also "shunned" the towering god-seat, through being "too shy" to live there (Hymn to Hermes). And, as we shall see, Hermes was often away from Olympus, both as a messenger of the gods and on his own behalf.

(It might be argued that Pan actually precedes the foundation of Olympus – he is certainly reckoned to be among the oldest of the gods (Allen 1904), being as he is a personification of various primal forces (or, may be thought of such, depending on how one views the gods).[25] If this were to be the case – and it is merely supposition – it's possible that he might see Olympus as a place that is "nice to visit, but you wouldn't want to live there"...)[26]

---

[23] Music as a genre, as an activity: this question is a general one, not one asking for commentary on the latest musical trends.

[24] Allen makes the pertinent point, in relation to the timing and place of the composition of the Hymn, that it is unlikely to have been Athenian in origin, or at least not to have been composed in the immediate aftermath of the battle of Marathon – if that were to be the case, surely some mention of the god's part in that victory would have been made? (Allen 1904; see also: Burkert 1985 on the timing of his cult in Athens)

[25] It is worth remembering that time simply does not work in a linear fashion for the gods... as Garland says, they are eternal but also have definite moments of beginning (Garland 1994).

[26] I'm aware that Merivale sees Pan as a "latecomer" and "second rate" god among Olympians. I just happen to disagree... (Merivale 1969, p. 1)

If we add this rustic picture – prancing among the mountain peaks, surrounded by nymphs[27] – to that at the outset of this section from Apuleius, we have a reinforced picture not just of a rural scene but of a pastoral divinity – both authors make clear the fact that Pan is a god, at the outset. (The fact of being a son of Hermes would not necessarily be enough to denote divinity, as plenty of gods fathered mortals.) While various (modern) authors might try to demote or devalue Pan, there is no way that he can be made less than god-like, if the ancient evidence is taken to be of any value at all. Particularly for the Arcadians, he was the god who provided, who ensured prosperity (Codellas 1945). (However, it seems unlikely that he was seen as the "all," (as Codellas suggests) even if it is possible to make this sort of pun on his name (Merivale 1969).)

The Hymn gives one of the reasons Pan roams over the hills – to watch over his sheep. This, again, is a family trait – Hermes was known to be a herdsman as well. This attribute of Pan's came in more than handy for the other Olympians, when Pan was able to disguise Kadmos (a hero) as a shepherd, and plotted with him to kill Typhoeus, who, in his war with the gods, had stolen the sinews of Zeus (Nonnus); not only was Pan the god of the shepherds, he understood them well enough to allow him to disguise someone as a shepherd in a convincing way. (This story, of course, adds weight to the idea that Pan was something other than a second rate, Johnny come lately among the Olympians.)

In fact, if we take the words of Zeus himself, Pan must be older than the leader of the gods – as Pan was the shepherd of Zeus' own nurse Amaltheia – herself a goat (Nonnus). Which means that Pan is older than Zeus, who presided over Pan's introduction (as a baby) to the gods on Olympus. (I refer the reader to my comments above about not imposing order on chaos.) There is, of course, the somewhat dubious authority of Herodotus to back up this claim to the antiquity of Pan – the

---

[27] For information about the nymphs, see (Larson 2001).

"father of history" has him as among the oldest gods known in Egypt, even if the Greeks see him as among the youngest (Herodotus 1972).[28]

All of which is very confusing to the modern mind. Perhaps we should concentrate on the fact of the shepherd-like qualities of the great god and move on?

Homeric Hymn to Pan – part the second

> Often he runs along shining distant mountains, and often he races down the mountain sides, killing wild beasts - so piercing is his eye.

This verse (these verses) introduce us to a side of Pan rarely mentioned in the modern literature about this god: Pan is not only a shepherd, guarding his flock, but also a hunter. While this image may not sit easily with various people who dislike the idea of hunting, Arcadians seem to have had few such scruples (and indeed, had little or no luxury for them: hunting and gathering were survival activities, not leisure sports).

Pan's aspect as a hunter seems to have been well known; certainly hunters were advised to ask for his help:

> Ye gods and goddesses all, who have protection of the fields, your altars offered kindly words: 'Whoever you are who come as a guest, you will hunt the hare along my path or any bird you seek: and whether you pursue your prize with rod or hound, summon me, Pan, from the crag to be your companion.' (Propertius)

Indeed, if we take the ancient visitor's guide to Greece as a basis, it was hunting that got Pan to Arcadia in the first place: "Pan, they say, visited Arcadia. Roaming from mountain to mountain as he hunted, he came at

---

[28] Herodotus gets round this discrepancy by assuming that the Greeks reckon the ages of the gods in question (Dionysus, Hermes and Pan) not from their actual births but from when the Greeks became aware of them – he plumps for the Egyptian dating himself.

last to Mount Elaios" (Pausanias, 8.42.1). (Of course, Pausanias is no more likely to tell his readers who the ubiquitous "they" are than the modern tabloid press.) According to Nonnus, Pan is known as a hunter, Agreus, and "was well versed in the beast-slaying sport of the hunt." (Nonnus, 14.67)[29]

This is, of course, a different side to the goat foot god than that seen above: goats are remarkable for many things, but hunting is not one of them; as others have noted, it doesn't take a great deal of skill to sneak up on a blade of grass...or most of the other things that goats are wont to eat.

And in fact, this view of Pan shows a different side from that normally portrayed. He is described in these passages as swift and skillful, an image which belies even some of the early depictions of him as heavy set and ungainly. Though when one considers how much of his time he spent running about on hills (going by the Hymn) and running after nymphs (going by many other tales), the swiftness might well make more sense.

These passages (though admittedly not the Hymn itself) also introduce two other associations for Pan: that of hounds, and the (far more important) companionship of Dionysus (which we will take up below).

Pan is known as a breeder of dogs, and even gives hounds to Artemis (Callimachus, 86). Dogs, of course, make sensible companions for a hunter. Nonnus calls Pan a breeder of hounds (Nonnus, 16.185); indeed, they are seen as the hounds of the "invincible" Pan (36.196) by the same author.

This is an interesting association, for all that it is a sensible one. There are a number of hounds and associations with hounds in the Greek tales, but perhaps fewer than one might expect. Artemis, of course, has hounds (and bears...) for hunting, as does Dionysus. Hecate is associated with a black hound, various monsters are referred to as "hounds of Zeus" at times, Heracles has to deal with a rather overly

---

[29] It may be worth noting that the sources cited for Pan's huntsmanship span the range from that of the Hymns through to Nonnus, in the 5th century CE; the association of Pan with the hunt is longstanding.

endowed (in terms of heads) hound, and of course Actaeon comes to a rather sad (and messy) end at the paws and jaws of his own pack of hounds. Yet, for those seen to hunt with hounds, there is a suggestion that those hounds (or some of them) were gifts of Pan. Does this again suggest that the goat-foot god is older than some myths would make him seem? The evidence is inconclusive and of course will remain so – but the point is interesting.

It's perhaps worth noting, at least in passing, that Pan is not entirely confined to the hills – he is also invoked or at least prayed to by sailors (fishermen)? Both Aeschulus (Persians) and Euripides (Iphegenia in Tauris) mention him in this guise.

Homeric Hymn to Pan – part the third

> Only in the evening when he lets go the hunt - then he makes sounds on his pipes of reed - playing a sweet deep song. And no bird can surpass him in song - not even she who when spring is full of flowers pours fourth her lament among the leaves singing with honey voice a mournful song.

> Then the clear-singing mountain nymphs roam around with him on their strong feet chanting by a spring of clear water while Echo on the mountain-top wails.

> The god now this side of the chorus - now that - or at times gliding into the midst of them - conducts the dancing feet, wearing the blood-red skin of a lynx upon his back; his heart delighting in the shrill songs in a soft meadow where crocuses and sweet-smelling hyacinths mix in with the grass wherever they like.

This section of the Hymn introduces us to a number of issues concerning Pan: his love of music and dance, his association with the nymphs, and Echo in particular, and his apparel (such as it is).

Pan's association with music is well known; even Justice herself hails him "chief of Satyrs in dance and song" (even if she does add to this the rather puzzling "most gallant of Athens' soldiers" (Lucian) – we shall return to this warrior aspect below). Revellers ask him to bestow a "benevolent smile" on their songs (Aristophanes, Thesmophoriazusae); those who linger near places sacred to him can "hear his pipes" (Pausanias, 8.36.8); Pan is called "melodious", plays for the wedding of a god, and for victorious warriors, etc. (Nonnus). He is asked to make music from his "sweet lips" fall in time to the choral words, and "about thee to the pulse of the rhythm let the inspired foot of these water-nymphs keep falling free;" his "supple lips" make music which entices the nymphs to dance (Mackail).

Pan is not supreme among the gods when it comes to music, however – at least not according to the contest staged between Apollo and Pan. According to Ovid, Pan's boast about his musical skills led to the contest, judged by Timolus. The contrasts between the gods could hardly be greater. Pan is described: "This old god sat down on his own mountain, and first eased his ears of many mountain growing trees, oak leaves were wreathed upon his azure hair and acorns from his hollow temples hung" – very unlike Apollo, whose "...golden locks were richly wreathed with fresh Parnassian laurel; his robe of Tyrian purple swept the ground; his left hand held his lyre, adorned with gems and Indian ivory." Needless to say, the award is made to Apollo, rather than to Pan (Ovid, 11.194).[30] One might see this as a triumph of the civilized and urbane over the raw forces of nature: but we have no evidence that the Greeks thought this way. I suspect they are more likely to think, simply, that Apollo played the lyre more pleasingly than Pan played his pipes...

Having said that, however, it should be noted that various Greek sources – a good number of fragments among them – laud Pan as a dancer; as an adornment to the chorus, as singing god-inspired songs, a

---

[30] Midas, however, disagrees with the judgement, and suffers for it:

> The Delian god forbids his stupid ears to hold their native human shape; and, drawing them out to a hideous length, he fills them with gray hairs, and makes them both unsteady, wagging at the lower part: still human, only this one part condemned, Midas had ears of a slow-moving ass (Ovid, 11.194).

...thus proving the truth of the point made in the introduction: do not anger the gods. (See also the version recorded by Hyginus (Hyginus, Fabulae, CXCI.))

fine dancer, (and with a blond beard!); his tune is well known and recognized (Nonnus, 17.69); his playing has "changeable, sweet notes" (Nonnus, 29.284); he is hailed as "melodious" (Nonnus, 45.174); he loves the dance (Aeschylus, Eumenides, 449). Pan, as other pastoral gods, acts as chorus leader of the nymphs (Larson 2001); he is the "dancemaker" for the gods (Sophocles, Ajax, 695).

And, of course, Pan's particular instrument – the Pan pipes, or syrinx – provides the link between his love of music and his association with the nymphs, as the syrinx is named for one of Pan's (fairly frequent, it would seem) unsuccessful attempts to "make sweet music" with a nymph.

Syrinx often "escaped the gods" to go abroad in the forest – having vowed virginity, she dressed in the manner of Diana, even to carrying a bow made of horn. As was almost bound to happen, she attracted the attention of Pan, "whose head was girt with prickly pines" (as opposed to the laurels of Apollo?). We don't have a record of what Pan said to her, merely that it wasn't effective – she scorned "the prayers of Pan" and ran from him – till the shores of a lake (big enough to have waves on it!) stopped her. Rather than submit to Pan, she asked "her sister Nymphs to change her form"[31] – a not uncommon way of getting out of this kind of trouble (or indeed, of being punished) in Greek myth. As Pan reaches for her, triumphant, he find that he holds only a handful of hollow reeds, which produce music as he sighs across them. In a phrase reminiscent of the poet as much as the lusty lover, he proclaims (at least, according to Ovid), "Forever this discovery shall remain a sweet communion binding thee to me" (Ovid, 1.689-712). While it is notable that some of the early depictions of Pan don't show the pipes, many of the later ones do – and it becomes almost synonymous with the god as time goes on.

But – what sort of being was Syrinx?

---

[31] This story places a good deal of power in the hands of the nymphs – see below.

35

The nymphs are regular, if not overly frequent, inhabitants of Greek myth.[32] Their exact classification is the stuff of debate, because, as above, it simply does not seem to have occurred to the Greeks to make such a distinction. Larson refers to them in terms of divinity, and so shall I.

Nymphs are quintessentially associated with water – particularly free flowing spring water, and especially that found on mountains and/or in caves (a cave on a mountain being triply blessed).

The Greeks seem to have taken two views (at least) of nymphs: either as virtuous maidens (and there is linguistic evidence for this view), attached to the train of the maiden goddess Artemis (or dedicated to her, or having another reason to refuse congress with males outright), or as something akin to spirits of freedom and fertility.[33] While it might be thought that it is only the latter with whom we need concern ourselves (after all, we're talking about Pan), that would not be the case. In fact, we seem to know more of his encounters with the nymphs who weren't keen on the types of interaction he... proposed... than those who enjoyed his particular form of revelry.

Nymphs seem to be a constant in Greek thought – already by the time of Homer their characteristics were fairly well set. They congregate around certain places, and where they are, there is very, very likely to be

---

[32] I am indebted to the work of Jennifer Larson on the nymphs (Larson 1997; Larson 2001); other sources will be cited, but so much is informed by Larson's work that citations would be overwhelming. (Errors, of course, remain my own.) It should also be noted that while they may be related, the nymphs are not the same deities as the Charites or Graces, with whom Pan is at times associated (Haldane 1968).

[33] While it is entirely possible that this is a modern reading, it must be made against what we know of the lives of the women of Greece. While it is clearly impossible for the vast majority of women to have lived the secluded lives of the Athenian maiden/matron of good family (after all, what distinguishes the working classes is the fact that they must *work* for a living, and slaves had no such luxury as seclusion), it is also true that from what we know, women lived an even more restricted life than men of the time (Shorter 1983; Alic 1986; Lefkowitz 1986; Brut-Zaidman 1990; Pantel 1990; Scheid 1990; Schied 1990; Sissa 1990; Thomas 1990; Lefkowitz and Fant 1992; Bullough 1993; Anderson and Zissner 1999; Pratt 2000).

music and/or dancing. There are shrines to them, even if at least one of those shrines is taken over by Pan (or his cult) (Ovid, 14.513); such shrines as remained to them were under the protection of no less god than Dionysus (Euripides, Bacchae). Pan seems to have made his home – or been made at home – in the non-Arcadian shrines of the nymphs, which tended to be caves or cave-like, sometimes taking them over from the nymphs (Ovid, 14.44). In Arcadia, however, this seems not to have happened; there, in his homeland, Pan has his own sanctuaries. (Whether associated with Dionysus or Pan, however, the nymphs were not to be offered wine.)

Pan is depicted engaging with the nymphs in four ways. The first is that recalled by bit of the Hymn above – leading their chorus, dancing with them or providing the music for their dance, or even, as in the Hymn, acting as rustic choreographer for them.

Secondly, the nymphs aid Pan as prophet. This is the Pan who is perhaps the most foreign to the modern, western mind. We are used to the lusty Pan, to Pan the musician, even to Pan the source of terror – but Pan as prophet? We associate prophecy with Apollo and his shrines – after all, who has not heard of Delphi?[34] Pythian Apollo? Yet if we listen to our forefathers, we would know that not only did Pan (and/or his father) initiate Apollo into the art of music, Pan it was who taught the golden god the "mantic art" (Apollodorus, 1.22-23). Pan was apparently known as prophetic from birth (Nonnus, 14.67); Pausanias informs us that there is a sanctuary of Pan in Arcadia, where it is said that "in the old days" the god gave oracles, with Erato (a nymph) as his prophetess (Pausanias, 8.37.11).

Prophecy is not something we, in this day and age, normally associate with the goat foot god – we tend to rely on the more usual ideas of him as sexually very active and possibly inspiring panic. Perhaps this is because we have a slightly different view of what prophecy is…?

---

[34] Certainly the original followers of Pan had done so – the Spartans left most of them alone due to a Delphic oracle. Sparta attacked only Tegea, and even there, the oracle was ambiguous enough that the Spartans, sure of the victory, ended up wearing the very chains they had brought to enslave the Tegeans (Herodotus).

The Greeks don't seem to have expected answers to prophetic questions to be overly clear, and in that, they were not disappointed (Garland 1994). Pan, along with Apollo and other gods, was a healing god with temples which provided those seeking his help a place to sleep – his help came often enough in the form of dreams (which might, or might not, need to be interpreted for the dreamer). Prophetic answers don't seem to have come from the gods in terms of "Tuesday would be good for a war" or "Marry Hypolutus not Hippocrates" – but were far more guarded and far less clear... which might accord more with the idea of the nature god that Pan was?

The third way in which Pan interacts with the nymphs is not mentioned in the Hymn, other than obliquely (as a reference to the pipes). The Hymn may be silent on Pan's sexual adventures: much of the rest of ancient writing about him is not. More often than not, nymphs are portrayed as spurning his advances: Syrinx we have seen; Pitys has much the same issues and suffers a fate somewhat similar, being transformed into a tree (Nonnus, 2.92, 42.257).

Opinion seems to be divided as to whether or not Pan had more luck with another nymph, Echo (doomed to chattering incessantly by Hera, and reduced to nothing but a voice because Narcissus refuses her love (Ovid, 3.350)). In one source, they are clearly a couple, as Pan is described as "sitting... holding the mountain deity[35] Echo in his arms" (Apuleius, 5.25). Nonnus, however, says that she feared Poseidon, having "escaped" Pan (Nonnus, 6.257).

There is, however, a more general feeling that the nymphs – other than the named ones who run from him – join Pan in the sexuality that is part of his ... work? ... as a pastoral, agrarian god; the sense seems to be that the god's engagement in sexual activity will have an effect on the fertility of the land. Perhaps it is *only* those nymphs who refuse his attentions, who stand out from the crowd?

Certainly Pan seems to have had enough success with some of the nymphs to father progeny. Ovid tells us that Acis was a great joy to his

---

[35] Which goes some way to answering the question asked above about the exact status of nymphs...

mother Symaethis (a nymph) and his father, Pan (Ovid, 13.750). Crenaeus is cited as the son of Pan and the nymph, Ismenis (Statius, 9.318).

Finally, while we will discuss Pan's parentage in more detail below, it's worth noting here that there are ancient authorities who see him as nymph-born (Nonnus; Apollodorus 1999).

The only other possibly discordant note in this section of the Hymn is the attire of the god – a lynx skin, described as "blood red."

Yet, what else would be more appropriate for a god whom, as we have seen, was a lord of the hunt? There are few, if any, tales in which Pan is seen as the friend of animals, per se (though it must be admitted that there are sculptures which show him having at the very least an... intimate relationship with some of them). Yes, he is portrayed as a protector of flocks, but almost always in terms of protecting at least semi-domesticated flocks: he protects not animals for themselves, but livestock, that is, the property of those who honour him.[36] It is certainly true that the lynx skin is a common feature in ancient paintings of Pan.

Homeric Hymn to Pan – part the fourth

They sing of the blessed gods, and high Olympos; they tell of Hermes who brings luck beyond all others - how he is the swift messenger of all the gods; and how he came to Arcadia, with its many springs - mother of the flocks, where Kyllene is - the sacred place of the god.

And there, though he was a god, he tended the sheep with their shaggy fleece for a mortal man; all because there came over him and intensified melting longing to lie with the nymph with the beautiful hair, daughter of Dryops.

It ended in joyous marriage.

---

[36] And, as such, is to be found (and honoured) in grottoes – for the grotto is the place where the shepherd/goatherd takes his flock in necessity, that is, it is a place of refuge not for wild animals but for those who interact with humans (Borgeaud 1988).

And in the house she gave birth to a dear son for Hermes who
from the first was marvellous to look upon with goat's feet and
two horns, loving noise, and laughing sweetly.

Here, at last, we come to the actual origins of the goat foot god – his
parentage, at least. It's worth noting that this retelling of the birth of
Pan is inserted into the Hymn as a part of the song of the nymphs: they
sing of the birth of Pan, to please Pan, perhaps?

And of course, they are singing of Olympus. Olympus was (and is)
the highest mountain in Greece, and therefore, a sensible place to
imagine as the home of the gods, or at least some of the gods.[37] While it
is generally thought that Pan did not abide on Olympus, he seems
always to have been welcome there, and among those who did live on
the mountain. (It must be said that it is difficult to imagine Pan confined
even to the most luxurious dwelling place – sooner or later, the lure of
the chase (deer, game, nymphs...) would call him from the dining couch
to the hills.)

The subject of this part of the Hymn, however, is not the cloud
wreathed home of the gods but one god in particular – "swift footed"
Hermes, the messenger of the gods. As he is generally reckoned to be
Pan's father (Cicero; Plato, Cratylus; Brown 1977; Apollodorus 1999;
Richardson 2003) (although not all ancient sources agree, most of them
do[38]), it is worth spending at least some time examining just what and
who this god was.

---

[37] Not all of the Greek gods resided on Olympus, of course – as we shall see in
our discussion of Pan himself. Moreover, not all aspects of the Olympian gods
would have been at home on the peak: see the discussion below re: chthonic
gods.

[38] Brown points out that there are at least eighteen ancient variants on the
parentage of Pan; Borgeaud would have it fewer, but still as high as fourteen
(and Hyginus; cf. the tradition enshrined in Herodotus; Brown 1977; Borgeaud
1988). It is possible that Aeschylus trod a middle road and claimed that there
was more than one Pan – one, a son of Zeus and Kallisto, the second, a son of
Cronos (and thus the brother of Zeus) (Borgeaud 1988). Either of these lineages
would be interesting, to say the least – for the second would explain why, in
Arcadia at least, Pan is given honours equal to those of Zeus, and also why Pan

Perhaps the most commonly known attribute of Hermes was his state as messenger of the gods – he was sent by Zeus to find Demeter when her mourning caused famine on the earth (Richardson 2003).[39] The relationship between Zeus and Hermes is generally at the least a cordial one, as befits father (Zeus) and son (Ovid, Met.; Hesiod; Homer, Odyssey) (and this, of course, makes Pan a grandson of Zeus, if this genealogy is followed). The Homeric Hymn to Hermes (one of the longer of the Hymns) makes it fairly clear that even from birth this god was more than a handful – within the space of his first day, he had escaped his swaddling bands and stolen sheep from Apollo (thereby beginning the family issues with the mantic god, perhaps?). Apollo of course is none too pleased and doesn't believe the excuse that no babe in arms could have stolen full grown cattle – only the creation of the lyre from a passing turtle appeases him (see notes above about Pan supposedly teaching Apollo about music – again, keeping things in the family, at least mythologically?). It is worth noting that Hermes supposedly slaughtered 12 of the cattle, and sacrificed them to the gods, thereby being credited at times with having invented worship.[40]

In fact, the Hymn tells us a great deal about Hermes – not only does he invent the lyre, he brings fire to humans through fire sticks. (The Hymn is silent on whether or not he invented theft, but as Apollo has a word for the idea and doesn't have to explain it to anyone, the likelihood is that Hermes was not the first thief.) We learn that he was conceived in a cave, to a nymph with beautiful hair (and thus, when he finds Pan's mother, finds a "girl just like dear old mum"?).

---

was involved in the battle against the Titans in quite the way he was (see below).

[39] Thus, a motif of the rustic (the acorn eater) finding or at least pointing the way toward civilisation (Demeter, grain, agriculture)? Possibly....

[40] The logos-oriented mind will now be attempting to construct a list of those 12 gods which does not include Hermes (he would hardly have sacrificed to himself) or Pan (who, after all, could hardly have been on the scene quite yet). The mythos oriented mind, on the other hand, might well be concentrating on the concept of sacrifice, and the connection between being a messenger, a thief, and the creator of sacrificial ritual...

The Hymn sets out the character of Hermes quite clearly:[41]

> She [Maia] gave birth to a son who was versatile and full of tricks, a thief, a cattle-rustler, a bringer of dreams, a spy by night, a watcher at the gate, one who was destined to bring wonderful things to light among the immortal gods.

Hermes lives up to these epithets almost immediately, by wriggling out of his swaddling clothes, finding a tortoise and creating the lyre, finding Apollo's cattle and stealing them, returning to his mother to promise her great things, and then lying through his teeth to an enraged Apollo about the fate of the cattle... and eventually even lies to their mutual father, Zeus, when the aggrieved Apollo takes his younger brother before the council of the gods.

Zeus, however, is cannier than his elder son, and orders the younger to reveal the hiding place of the cattle – which Hermes (apparently judging that this has gone far enough for safety) does straight away. Apollo recovers all but two of his cows – two, however, have been sacrificed to the gods (see below).

Shocked at the strength shown in such a sacrifice, Apollo decides to bind Hermes with ropes – to no avail. It is only with the playing of the newly invented lyre that the brothers come to some accord. Their father declares that Hermes will be the lord of the wild animals and flocks, and the only consecrated messenger to Hades. The Hymn ends with what may well be a timely note:

> And now he mingles with everyone, mortal and immortals alike.
> A few he helps, but he endlessly beguiles the race of human beings in the darkness of the night.

While this is not the place for a long excursus on the god with winged sandals, there are elements of his story as portrayed here and elsewhere

---

[41] Again, it is worth remembering that the Greeks seem to have felt no need to be particularly polite *about* their gods, even if they were more careful when actually interacting with them. They saw no issue with calling a lecher a lecher or, in the case of Hermes, calling a thief, a thief (Garland 1994).

which are useful to note in relation to his son (if indeed Pan is his son – but for the most part, we will take the general tradition of Pan's parentage as given, even while noting the odd discordant voice).

There are two main areas to examine: places of congruence and places of difference.

The similarities outweigh the differences (as one might expect?). Both Pan and Hermes are the sons of the pairing of a god and a nymph (at least according to the Hymns); both seem to have been remarkably precocious from birth; both are associated with caves, nature and animals; both are associated with prophecy and divination.

In fact, there is really only one main difference, which is expressed twice in the Hymn relating to Hermes, once openly and once in a more roundabout manner. As seen above, Hermes is instituted as the messenger to Hades; he is known to antiquity not only as a thief and messenger, but also as a psychopomp, one who leads the dead to the underworld (Luck 1999); he is one of the chthonic gods associated with the dark, with the earth (Faraone 2004). And early on in the Hymn, when he prepares a sacrifice (and thus is credited with the institution of worship), he does not partake of any of the meat from the sacrificed animals (much as he wishes to). Rather, he incinerates them, in a holocaust – the type of sacrifice generally associated with the chthonic, dark[42] gods, rather than the Olympians.

One of the remarkable things about Pan, on the other hand, is the (almost? I have found no evidence...) complete lack of any chthonic side to his cult or beliefs about him,[43] in the sense of having to do with the dead. There are no stories of him leading the dead, of his relations with Hades – the closest he comes is the very-far-removed finding of Demeter as she mourns the missing Kore (Persephone). He has no contact with shades, or with death per se – although his own death was (perhaps) announced, as we shall see, he seems to have no chthonic side at all (in

---

[42] "Dark" here is used as a reference to lack of light, rather than to any supposed moral opposition between "light" and "dark;" chthonic gods tended to be worshipped at night, and to have as sacrifices dark or black animals.

[43] I am indebted to Chris Naden for this insight.

the sense of dealing with the dead or the dark), as opposed to so many of the other Greek Gods. He is not a god of the dead, a guide of the dead, he has no association with the dead. He is quintessentially a god not only of the living but of life itself – particularly of the creation of new life, that is, of fertility; in the words of Burkert, Pan "…embodies the uncivilized power of procreation which nevertheless remains indispensable and fascinating for civilized life" (Burkert 1985, 172).

On the other hand, if we take "chthonic" back to its root meaning (*chthonios*), "of (or in, or under) the earth," then perhaps Pan is closer to being a chthonic god. But he is still not there – for he is not a god of the *earth* so much as he is a god of "that which is upon the earth" – particularly the earth's animal life. He is a fertility god (Merivale 1969), but almost entirely of animals rather than plants.[44]

And this, even to his appearance, given above as "with goat's feet and two horns, loving noise, and laughing sweetly." Even at birth, he shows an "animal" nature, or at least an animal form.

Homeric Hymn to Pan – part the fifth

> But his mother jumped up and ran away, as soon as she caught sight of his harsh face and this thick beard - she was terrified and left the child alone.

Pan's mother is not named in the Homeric Hymn; she is known merely as the "daughter of Dryops," and by the fact that she had beautiful hair. (Other authors name her as Penelope – either the wife of Odysseus, who conceives through mating with all of her suitors or one suitor in particular, or a different Penelope, who was confused with the more famous queen (Apollodorus).)

---

[44] It could, of course, be argued that any Arcadian is chthonic by nature – as they were reckoned to be "autochthonous," that is, tracing their ancestry back to one who was born of the earth itself (Borgeaud 1988). However, this again isn't quite what the word means.

A mother abandoning her child seems heinous to us,[45] but we must question whether or not it would seem so to the audience of the Hymn. The debates about infanticide – how often it was practiced, and for what reasons – have been going on in scholarly circles for quite some time (see, for example: Bennett 1923; Cameron 1932; Patterson 1985; Ingalls 2002). One factor which seems fairly certain, however, is that many, many babies who were carried, were not born alive, and that of those who were live births, many did not become toddlers, much less adults: infant mortality rates may well have been as high as one in two in the classical world (Ingalls 2002); this is not to say that infanticide would be either an easy decision for parents to take or a common one, but one might argue that frequent infant death from other causes might in some way desensitise society to the practice. (One might, of course, equally argue that a high infant mortality rate would lead to all surviving infants being seen as precious.) And as Patterson points out, in demanding quantitative evidence, we may be putting too great a strain on sources which were never designed to be used in this way (Patterson 1985) – another instance of attempting to approach mythos through the lens of logos, perhaps?

However often it may have happened, it would be difficult to argue that abandonment of children was *unknown* in Greece – after all, the practice figures in the histories of some of the gods and heroes themselves. So the actions of the "daughter of Dryops" would, at least, have had a precedent.[46] And, of course, she does not call for the exposure of the child – one might well suppose from the wording of the

---

[45] Harrison holds that Pan was abandoned not by his mother but by his nurse (Harrison 1926). However, the Hymn is fairly clear that it is the daughter of Dryops who runs away – depending on the translation of the word used, of course.

[46] The actions also seem to indicate a male author; as one who has been through a difficult labour (and what else could the birth of a being with horns *and* hooves – sharp at both ends! – be, other than difficult?), I suspect that there was at the very least a time lag of some hours between the birth and the "jumping up and running away" – something a mother might well have pointed out or known...

Hymn (see next section) that she knew well that Hermes was already pleased enough with their son to see to his well-being.

However, it is not the nymph's actions here which are of interest, but rather, the possible reaction of the infant to those actions.

We have seen that Hermes, at least, was more than capable of rational thought, clear speech and decisive action from the day of his birth. It might not be too much of a leap, then, to suppose that Pan was at least aware of the fact that his mother was no longer near him; even if that realisation took some time, it seems probable rather than not that Pan grew up (for whatever that word may mean for an ageless god) knowing that his mother had abandoned him early on.

It has been suggested that what Pan actually represents is not the drive to mate, not the drive to satisfy a sexual urge, but rather a need: a profound and existential need for unity (Hillman and Roscher 1972). He seeks union – unity – copulation – almost constantly, either through sex (hence the tales not only of his loves but of his pursuits), or through physical activity leading to other forms of union (dance, music). While not wishing to impose such a structure on the Homeric Hymn (which after all, says nothing of the kind), it is perhaps not too much of a stretch to connect the post-birth maternal abandonment of Pan with this desire for (re)union? This is speculation at best – but interesting speculation, nonetheless.

To return to the words of the Hymn, it is clear that even from the outset, Pan's features are those of an adult – hence the beard. In fact, in the oldest representations of him, Pan is a man if not in his physical prime, then just past it – a man of middle age, still powerful and able to dance and leap, but certainly no callow youth (and, indeed, no beauty by the standards of the day). There seems to have been something about Pan which, to the Greek mind at least, proclaimed not youth but powerful, full adulthood.

Homeric Hymn to Pan – part the sixth

Quickly Hermes who brings the luck took him in his arms, accepting him. And happy in his heart beyond measure was the god.

46

So quickly wrapping his son in the warm skins of mountain hares, he went to the home of the immortal gods and he sat down beside Zeus and the other gods and showed them his boy.

Then all the immortal gods were glad in their hearts but most of all Bacchos Dionysos.

They called him Pan - because he delighted the hearts of all.

Whatever the actions of the "daughter of Dryops," it seems that the baby's father had a very different reaction to the remarkable birth. Hermes (here denoted as one who "brings good luck" rather than as the prince of thieves – both are apt, of course) is very pleased with his son, and "accepts him." For a society which practiced infanticide at least occasionally when babies were born with abnormalities, this acceptance takes on a greater significance than might otherwise be the case.

Foreshadowing the baby's life as a hunter, Hermes wraps him in the "warm skins of mountain hares" – warm because they have just been removed from their former owners? According to Hillman, this initiates the babe into the world of Eros, Aphrodite and the moon (Hillman and Roscher 1972); whether or not this is the case (and it seems a bit of a reach), it is in keeping with the livelihood of the father (shepherd) and the eventual lifestyle of the child.

And Hermes does what so many parents do as soon as they can after birth – he introduces the child to his extended family, starting with his father, Zeus. And all the gods were delighted with the babe, in particular, Dionysus.

Dionysus, the god of wine and viniculture, general pleasure and festivals, was no stranger to the concept of a rough start in life. Traditions vary as to exactly what happened in the early stages of his life, but all of them agree that things were far from easy: either he was born from the thigh of his father (sewn there as a 6 month foetus when his mother was incinerated due to the splendour of seeing her lover – Zeus – in all his glory), or he was torn apart by Titans and re-animated from his rescued heart (Hyginus, Fabulae).[47] Both stories lend credence to the title, "twice born," by which Dionysus is often known.

Pan and Dionysus are often depicted together: most of the time, Pan is one of the followers of, or the follower of, the other god. Pan is referred to as "most festive of all Dionysus' followers" by Lucian (Lucian); it was his love of loud noise and "riot" that caused him to be the "minister and companion" of Dionysus (Virgil). (Of course, Pan also shares with Dionysus the ability to inspire madness, though they use that ability in different ways, as we shall see.)

Pan is, in theory, Dionysus' nephew, but this relationship is rarely if ever referred to in descriptions of their encounters and escapades – and indeed, those encounters are far more often depicted than described.

According to the Hymn, Pan acquired his name – pan meaning "all" – because he delighted all the gods on Olympus. However, it would seem that this is backwards reasoning, or a clever play on words, rather than accurate linguistic history; it's far more likely that Pan's name comes from the same word that gives us "pastoral" – and which signifies the herdsman (Boardman 1997). Whatever the derivation of his name, however, there must be some sense in which Pan does mean all – in that, as we have seen, Pan is the god of life and that which lives....

This first section has used the Homeric Hymn as a structure for discussion of the goat foot god, and has served us well in that manner. However, as noted at the outset, there are elements of the ancient beliefs about Pan which are not covered by the Hymn; it is to these we turn now.

---

[47] It is interesting that while Dionysus falls afoul of the rift between the Olympians and the Titans, Hermes and Pan can in some respects be said to heal that or be products of its healing – as Maia is a daughter of a Titan (Atlas) herself – so that Hermes has a Titan for a grandfather and Zeus for his father. Further, Rhea was the wife of Cronus – and Pan is at times seen as one of her companions.

What is this thing called "Panic"?

(And what does it have to do with sex?)

> The god Pan had driven the doubting city distraught, Pan fulfilling the cruel commands of the Mygdonian Mother,[48] Pan lord of the woodlands and of war, whom from the daylight hours caverns shelter; about midnight in lonely places are seen that hairy flank and the soughing leafage on his fierce brow. Louder than all trumpets sounds his voice alone, and at that sound fall helm and sword, the charioteer from his rocking car and bolts from gates of walls by night; nor might the helm of Mars [Ares] and the tresses of the Furiai [Erinyes], nor the dismal Gorgon from on high spread such terror, nor with phantoms so dire sweep an army in headlong rout. Sport it is to the god when he ravishes the trembling flock from their pens, and the steers trample the thickets in their flight. (Valerius Flaccus : 3.46)

This description, from the first century CE, is scary stuff: it presents a god of the dark[49] (who hides from not just noon, as we have seen above, but from all daylight),[50] a god who frightens people in almost every possible way. He carries out the orders of the Great Mother,[51] his very form is enough to strike fear, his voice is louder than instruments of war. He is more frightening even than the creatures who strike terror –

---

[48] We are told that the oak tree was sacred to Rhea, providing a clear link to Pan, of the land of the acorn-eaters (Apollodorus).

[49] This is, however, in keeping with Pan as an Arcadian god, as above – it was through an attack before moonrise that the Arcadians conquered their own land (Borgeaud 1988).

[50] This still does not, however, make Pan a chthonic god, in the sense of having to do with the dead (other than perhaps having a hand in turning the living into the dead...). As above, Pan's connection is to things of life, not death.

[51] Someone further from the fluffy conception of a celestial dispenser of cloud-baked cookies could not be imagined than Rhea...

the kindly ones[52] and the gorgon, and the phantoms who inhabit the night. For perhaps the only time in ancient literature, Pan is portrayed as causing harm to animals by causing flocks to stampede.[53]

This is not the Pan of the Homeric Hymn, or, rather, this is not the side of Pan made known in the Hymn. This is a much darker, all around more terrifying god – but not one who was unknown to the ancients.[54] Pan was known to cause the madness which takes his name, and in some texts, is actually credited with being warlike himself, although he is seen as a warrior himself only in one text (Polyaenus)[55] for reasons we shall see.

Pausanius, typically, puts it clearly: "causeless panics are said to come from the god Pan" (Pausanias, 10.23.7). This may be because people attributed to Pan things which happened apparently for no reason – and that, because noise and brouhaha were already attributed to the god whom "one must not approach in silence" (Suidas, Panikoi deimati). When the enemy is roused in the middle of the night and, rather than taking the initiative and swooping down on the unsuspecting Greeks (or Athenians), takes to attacking their own comrades – this is the work of the great god Pan. Confusion, indeed, to one's enemies, and what an elegant solution – he does not cause "his side" to be victorious, but rather staves off the battle entirely by causing

---

[52] Eumenides means, literally, "the kindly ones" – an epithet used to keep from drawing the attention of the Furies to the speaker. Or, indeed, writer...

[53] Yes, there **is** that statue from Herculaneum, which shows Pan involved in sexual activity with a goat. One might argue that this is causing harm to the animal, but that is hardly germane, as it is not literature, and quite frankly, the goat doesn't look overly perturbed. Considering the placement of the goat's hooves near the god's throat, the animal's displeasure, should it have arisen, might well have been demonstrated in a dangerous if not final way.

[54] Though he is, in relation to panic, almost always unseen, if not unknown, as we shall see.

[55] While it is true that there are more depictions of Pan in military garb than there are text descriptions of the same, this may well be merely a means of visually associating the goat foot god with the war-based panics for which he was famous (Borgeaud 1988).

a rout among the enemy, thereby saving the heroes from the tedium (and danger) of actually engaging them.

Pausanias, as well, relates the result of panic in war – encamped for the night, the Gauls begin to think that they can hear horses – soon the delusion spreads to all, and "panic" ensues. (Pausanias, 10.23.7)

At times, the panic is a more personal problem – Euripides insists that a character who is unable to tell an intelligible tale is "under the lash of trembling Pan" (Rhesus). Phaedra, when fainting and refusing food, is asked if she is possessed by Hecate or Pan (Hippolytus); Glauce's nurse assumes that her death throes are actually such god-possession and sends "a festal shout" heavenwards, as her mistress writhes in agony caused by Medea's gift of a poisoned robe (Medea). Even other gods may make use of this gift – Nonnus speaks of Dionysus "cracking" Pan's whip of madness to send an unbridled wife insane (Nonnus, 44.280). Considering the relationship which we have already seen between these two deities, such a sharing makes sense; it is as Dionysos' general that Pan makes his only appearance as a military deity in text (Polyaenus). Indeed, it would be interesting to speculate on the connection between the ecstasies of the maenads in their service to Dionysus and the panic induced by the goat foot god – or perhaps closer to panic would be the madness of Agave, this time induced by the slighted Dionysus.

In a tale that resembles closely that of the demise of Pentheus, Longus relates that Echo comes about her doom through spurning the great god. Angry at her refusal of his advances (and envious of her music), Pan causes the shepherds and goatherds to go mad and tear her limb from limb; her "still singing" limbs are flung all over the world (Daphnis and Chloe). Longus here highlights a side of Pan, or a view of Pan, that doesn't get a great deal of ancient press, and is perhaps the most sensible (if one can say that) proponent of the idea of Pan the warrior.

What does the story of Echo tell us? It may be worth reflecting on what an echo (note lower case) is. An echo is not a sound of its own – it is not proactive, it has no voice (it is not, to put it plainly and to pre-empt some of what will be seen in a later chapter, provocative). An echo is merely a re-sounding of something already said, already done – by the time an echo begins, the speaker has finished saying whatever it is that is echoed (even if the entire phrase overlaps the first part of the echo). The echo make no move of its own, no decision: it is entirely reactive. It is fleeting – the echo does not remain, it cannot (short of sophisticated sound equipment) be captured or held.

It is also distorted; by the very fact that we use the phrase, "it sounded like an echo" we acknowledge that echoes and "normal" sounds are not the same. An echo is faint, it lacks distinction, it melds separate sounds into one. It is notoriously difficult to reconstruct the original sounds by listening to an echo: an echo is a series of sounds, not a means of communication.

Yet the Greeks seem to have associated the echo, and indeed Echo herself, closely with Pan. Not only does he preside at her death (in at least one telling of the tale), at other times the two are seen entwined as lovers. Because they would have known both tales when using the (equivalent) word, an "echo" evoked all those feelings and ideas – hopeless love, rage, anger, hate, jealousy, loss – as well as love itself (Borgeaud 1988).

Yet many parts of this description – lack of distinction (soldiers fail to recognise comrades, mistaking them for the enemy), lack of normality or presence of otherness, reactivity rather than proactivity, hate, rage – all of these are also useful identifiers of panic, particularly the collective type of panic seen in military situations[56].

I've placed this motif here because it seems to fit under the heading of "panic" better than any other – and Longus makes the connection between Pan the soldier and panic more sensible than most (Merivale 1969). Longus has Pan "fight" (actually, reprimand) with those weapons one might expect: herds and music. Earlier (at least in terms of the chronology of myth, if not in terms of the dating of sources), Pan is thought to have assisted Zeus (his grandfather, according to the Hymn) in the battle against Cronus and the titans, again using sound but this

---

[56] Although it is a more tenuous point – hence its relegation to a footnote – Borgeaud makes the point that most if not all of the instances of military panic take place near a site which is sacred to Pan.

time his own voice, as a powerful weapon in defence of those who became the Olympians.

In the struggle with the Titans, Pan presents – for one of the few times in ancient literature – the character of a wily, trickster god. Having learned "the art of the deep" from his father, Pan lures Typhon with the promise of a fish feast – tricking the Titan into coming near enough to the shore of the sea for Zeus to kill him with thunder bolts and lightning (Oppian). Earlier (one presumes) in the battle, Pan has suggested to his companions that they transform themselves into the likenesses of beasts to deceive and avoid the monster (Hyginus, Fabulae); as we have seen above, this same author in another work holds that the transformations came about through fright rather than guile (Hyginus, Astronomica). Zeus was only able to do the monster in, of course, because Pan (or his son, Agipan) had returned to him his sinews, stolen by Typhon and sewn up in the skin of a bear (Apollodorus).

The most famous instance of Pan's forays into war, of course, is that which we still commemorate in the Olympic games as well as thousands of other times a year, whenever a marathon is run. Well, to be absolutely accurate, we commemorate the travels of Philippides from Marathon to Athens – however, it was while he was en route that the goat foot god made it plain that he was on the side of the Athenians (Herodotus, Book 6 ch. 105).

> Philippides went on to say that near Mount Parthenius he had been met by Pan, who told him that he was friendly to the Athenians and would come to Marathon to fight for them. This deity, then, has been honored for this announcement. (Pausanias, Attica 28 4)

This intervention is given as the reason for the temple to Pan in Athens – a temple or sacred area which might well need some explanation, as Pan and the settled life in Athens might well seem antithetical. Perhaps it was a constant reminder that civilization is merely a veneer?[57] At any

---

[57] Or, more prosaically, that the good citizens of Athens (that is, those men who could afford to do so) might well spend a reasonable amount of time not in the city at all but on country estates, and therefore, honouring the god of the wilds might simply be the prudent thing to do?

rate, according to Lucian, the temple was certainly there, and established enough that Pan himself was liable to pay taxes to the city "like any other naturalized foreigner;" he is addressed (with something far removed from seriousness, it must be said) as "most gallant of Athens' soldiers" (Lucian 1905). Wilson suggests that it is this incident which led to Pan being associated with war and soldiering – a plausible, if unprovable idea (Wilson 2004).

We are not told – by any of these authors – how exactly Pan "fought" in favour of the Athenians. While it may be a bit of a stretch to assume that he aided them here in the same way as he "attacked" the Gauls, it is not an unreasonable assumption. We know from other sources that Pan was fleet of foot (cf. citations above about Pan as hunter), and one can assume bodily strength, if nothing else, from the work he undertakes as a goat and sheep herder, as well that of one to whom games were dedicated (Wilson 2004). However, nowhere is he said to have undertaken training in weaponry or the arts of war; he is rarely if ever pictured with swords or arrows. Is it not more likely that he would choose those tools which were already familiar to him and had worked well enough in the past – that is, panic, induced by either an irrational fear (of things that go "thump!" in the forest or wild areas at night), or through a cacophonous voice?

To go further afield from what is actually recorded in the ancient texts, one might see in Pan, and in his presence among the more "citified" residents of Olympus, a constant reminder that the nature of both humans and the gods is not a single sided one: the same Pan who presides over the brutal murder of Echo, persuades Psyche to continue living, in spite of the sorrow she faces; the same god who pursues Syrinx relentlessly, seems to carry the pipes which she becomes as a constant reminder of what might have been (Diotima 2005). As Borgeaud points out, the experience of Pan is one we all understand (Borgeaud 1988). As we have seen above, this also relates to Pan's status as the Lord of Arcadia – which balances the love of music against the conception of being ever slightly more primitive than the rest of Greece (Borgeaud 1988).

Larson makes an interesting, if more or less off the cuff, remark about "panic sexuality" – that is, "futile" sexuality as exhibited by Pan and the nymphs (Larson 2001, 155). I'm unclear as to why this sexuality should be futile – certainly Pan is reckoned to be a father at times (hence an unfutile but indeed, fertile sexuality).[58] Borgeaud agrees with this estimation, and indeed suggests that Pan is infertile (in spite of clear evidence in some myths of his paternity). However, it could well be that Pan's loves are "futile" in the sense that quite often, it seems, the object of his desires manages to elude him – generally at a fairly high cost to herself.

Borgeaud, I believe, comes closer to the truth when he speaks not of futile sexuality but rather of futile desire – for it is not the god's sexuality which is futile but his pursuit of sexual objects (Borgeaud 1988).

Borgeaud makes the point that Pan's sexuality is not, as it were, "within bounds" – that is, it is outside the societal norm, it does not fit within any of the generally accepted means of expression. Pan's love, or his attentions at the very least, represent almost everything that is antithetical to marriage in ancient Greek thought. In terms of understanding both panic and Pan's sexuality (panic sexuality), it is worth remembering the value placed on the family by the societies of ancient Greece.

Perhaps the first point to be made about the family or community is that it was, for the Athenians at least, a male enterprise: women were not officially members thereof, were not listed on the rolls of the groups which comprised it (Gould 1980). Of course they were present and there were laws to protect them (well, at least to protect their capacity to be the bearers of property from one family and one generation to another), but officially, they did not exist as separate actors (Johnstone 2003).

---

[58] The argument will be raised that this sentence sees sexuality as futile unless it results in offspring. While that is not an argument the author would concede, it is certainly true that fertility was an important aspect of the sexuality embodied by Pan and the nymphs who were, after all, pastoral deities first and foremost. And one might add that the ability to inspire panic seems to have been if not genetic then at least passed somehow from sire to son, "Eurymedon pursues [with the Thebans the army of the Seven Against Thebes], with armour rustic and uncouth and rustic weapons in his hand and native skill to arouse panic terrors - his sire was Pan." (Statius, 11.32)

Women were under the protection of men their entire lives: their fathers (or the eldest male in the kin group), then their husbands then their sons, or any combination thereof (Gould 1980; Lefkowitz 1986; Cohen 1989; Schaps 1989; Sissa 1990; Zaidman 1990; Duby&Perrot 1992; Brock 1994; Holland 1998; Roy 1999; Johnstone 2003).

Secondly, the family was, as Aristotle pointed out, the basic unit of the polis, of the city state (Politics). While that may seem a fairly basic point, it needs to be borne in mind, particularly in relation to panic sexuality. Combining these two points, that of the centralizing of power in the male and that of the family as the basic unit of the state, the fear inherent in disturbances of the family may become more understandable. A threat to the family, to the smooth running of the family, was a threat to the state – and while men could be to some extent expected to understand this (they had a stake in the state, after all), women were not actors on the larger stage. They were rather, as the famous speech of the father of the bride indicates, acted upon, "I give this woman for the ploughing of legitimate children" (Roy 1999).

In terms of panic sexuality, it's also worth noting that silence was the greatest, perhaps the only, adornment of a well born woman in public (Sophocles, Ajax); the main (only?) exception to this was in the ritual sphere, where women were expected to give voice to songs, hymns, ritual cries, the mourning wail, etc., in many rituals (Gould 1980).

So here we have all the components that lead to the concept mentioned above of "panic sexuality" – which I will suggest means not only "Pan-ic" sexuality (that is, sexuality as it relates to Pan himself and any partners with whom he interacts) but also "panic" sexuality (that is, sexuality or sexual encounters that happen while in or under the influence of panic).

We have Pan himself, as seen both in the Hymn and in the other sources mentioned; we have a basic understanding of the place of women in classical Greek society (unenfranchised, politically and legally non-existent, always under the protection of males, and responsible for the creation of the next generation of citizens); and we have looked at the concept of the family (as the basis for legitimate children, cf the quotation from Demosthenes below about the tripartite division among types of women). The final part of the puzzle is, as Borgeaud notes, the fact that no matter how distinguished a match might be made, no matter how willing or subservient the wife or how powerful the husband, without sexual desire, the marriage will not fulfill its goal – and it is here that Pan re-enters the picture, for sexual desire is his special province (Borgeaud 1988).

Unfortunately, as scholars have observed, it is very much a male view of that world we are presented (Gould 1980), as almost all of the voices that speak to us from that universe are male: where women are made to speak, they do so at the hands of male essayists, playwrights and philosophers.

> In Pan's case, it is excessive desire that opposed him to marriage and leads to the fragmentation and dispersion of his erotic objects. Pan's sexuality is crippled by glut; it is cut off from its object, which vanishes in the end (cf. Echo, Syrinx), by a desire so intense that it cannot establish a relationship with an objective purpose. (Borgeaud 1988, p. 84)

In the preceding chapter, we took the parentage of Pan to be that of the Hymn – that is, his father is taken to be Hermes, and indeed, this is the most common way of seeing the descent of the goat foot god.[59]

However, what if, as noted above, that parentage is not accepted? Is the association of panic with Pan more easily understood if he is not, indeed, the son of the urbane and reasonably sophisticated Hermes, after all?

There are two other main candidates for paternity – Zeus, and Zeus' own (generally accepted) father, Cronus. The first would place Pan among the first generation of Olympians (or those who became Olympians, once they had overthrown the previous rule of the Titans); the second would place him even more remotely, among the earlier group of deities in Greek thought – huge, lumbering, almost primal.

---

[59] It is worth reiterating – here as elsewhere – that the question of parentage may not be an "either/or" choice. This is not, after all, a human whose ancestry we discuss, and things lost in the mists of myth need not be tidy...

There is a certain attraction in this thought – at least in terms of dealing with certain aspects of Pan, panic among them. One can much more easily understand the concept of panic, of uncontrolled, unthinking fear, as attaching to the Titans than to the more "civilized" gods who follow them. The stories told about the possibilities of human sacrifice on Mt. Lykaion in Arcadia, and the resultant lycanthropy of those who partake of it (or re-enact it), (Augustine, CofG, 18.17; Pausanias; Porphyry; Ovid; Borgeaud 1988; Apollodorus, 3.8) also seems more closely aligned to a primal deity.

It would also make sense in terms of what Pan is, symbolically – a primal force, a primal urge, the need (it is more than a desire) for unity, for mating. He is also, it would seem, tied to the basic life force in the Arcadian region, to "that which causes to be" if we wish to wax philosophical about it. And, of course, as the text at the outset of this chapter shows, Pan was not unknown to that generation of deities.

However, in many other ways, it doesn't make a great deal of sense. Why would Pan join Zeus and the others in their battle against the Titans, if he were one of them or their progeny? Yes, the same could be said of Zeus, but he did rather have a bone to pick with Cronus... Moreover, descriptions and particularly depictions of Pan constantly mention or show his shortness of statue – very un-Titan-like. Perhaps most telling, however, is his fairly constant affiliation with Dionysus and Hermes – which would hardly have been the case were he a Titan himself – nor would those relationships be as they were, were Pan a contemporary of Zeus, indeed, a brother of Zeus (making him not the son/nephew of Hermes and Dionysus, respectively, but their uncle).

Pan seems, rather, to fit well into the generation, as it were, of the sons and daughters of Zeus – or their children (which is where the Hymn places him). He deals with humanity in much the way they do (capriciously, but at times kindly), and perhaps more telling, humanity deals with him in that way.

While it might be possible to make a rather strained argument that there is increasing sophistication among the Greek gods as the generations go on (and this does seem to be the case in the first couple of generations) and that therefore, Pan is obviously "earlier" than Hermes and Dionysus, the argument would be strained at best – it would need very pretty footwork indeed to show that Pan's panic belonged to an earlier, ruder generation than the madness which was seen as a gift of his uncle (or a punishment from same).

While this discussion of parentage may seem a bit of a distraction in a chapter on panic, it does illustrate the point that one cannot examine only one "bit" of a god or the tales about a deity – everything must be taken together. What one must not do, however, is expect that final "everything" to make clear, logical, non-contradictory sense.

If this was the goat foot god in his ancient setting, how did humans relate to him? What was the cult of Pan like, who participated and why?

We will begin our examination of the cult of Pan – as usual with such things – by looking at definitions; we'll then move on to look at the elements of the cult (where, and what), then at other influences on the cult of Pan, such as the other divinities who were honoured with him. This will set the stage for an examination of a more modern Pan...

Perhaps the first thing here is to define "cult" as it is being used in this chapter. Anthropologically and theologically, "cultus" (Latin: cultus) denotes a system of belief that brings humans into relation with the divine (however that may be defined) or with beings of higher-than-human status – thus, the medieval "cults" of Mary and the saints. It is in this sense, rather than in the sense of "cult" as a group viewed as deviant by the mainstream, that the term is being used of the worshippers of Pan. As we shall see, it appears indeed that "the mainstream" (if by that we can mean the upstanding citizens of classical Greece) were if not enthusiastic practitioners of the cult of Pan, then certainly vouchsafed that cult a presence and practice in their midst.[60]

But it didn't start there – it would seem that the cult of Pan, like the goat god himself, begins in the countryside, in Arcadia: and it seems to have begun at about the time people there began to try to tame the landscape around them (Allen 1904; Codellas 1945). Taking into consideration all we've seen about Pan up till now, this beginning makes a great deal of sense.

---

[60] Though the present work is not particularly concerned with the cult of Pan as presented in the eternal city, it is perhaps worth pointing out that the goat foot god was certainly worshipped in Rome; and while it is true that Rome was a fairly benevolent mixing pot of religions, not all of them were happy admixtures - and some, such as the cult of Isis and the religion of the Jews (not to mention the Christians), were actively suppressed (Moehring 1959).

Pan is, if nothing else, liminal; he may well be described (as we shall see even more clearly below) as a walker between worlds.[61] Always associated with the wild, he interacts with humans; he is not the lord of the wild but rather of *human interaction* with the wild: he is part goat, a domesticated animal (for whatever value "domesticated" can ever have when applied to goats);[62] he is called upon by shepherds and goatherds, to aid them in their tasks of dealing with animals; he is the god of hunters, not of the hunted. So, as people began to take control of the wilds, to domesticate them (or at least make them a place in which to be domestic), they turned to a deity who was liminal – between states – half animal, half man; a deity, moreover, ideally suited to the task at hand.

French calls the domestication of nature an exercise of "power over" (French 1985). And this is quintessentially what Pan represents: the attempt to apply power over, to gain control over. Note that I say that this is the *attempt* to gain power over, rather than the attainment: as we have seen, he is rarely successful when he seeks to enforce his erotic will on women.

And Pan can impose the loss of power, in panic: one of his gifts is the removal of control.

Both of these movements: the attempt to control, and dealing with the aftermath of the loss of that control, would have been the daily stuff of those who first honoured Pan: the domestication of previously wild animals, the attempt to raise foodstuff on relatively unresponsive soil, hunting... these are all movements of control. Yet sheep and goats break the bounds of their steading, floods and fires destroy crops and homes. The Arcadians were well aware of their *lack* of power: is it any wonder they were so close to a god who, though almost always depicted as a powerfully built man, so often fails in his attempts to impose his will?

---

[61] Well, yes, perhaps it would be better to represent Pan as a *runner* or *dancer* between worlds, but the liminality of the exercise remains.

[62] Or cats...

And indeed, that seems to be what the cult of Pan was about: the earliest information we have about it, shows that Pan was regarded as the god of hunters and herders (Merivale 1969). The spoils of the hunt, and sometimes the means of the hunt (including a dog, which was later redeemed as it was needed), as well as goats from the flock were offered to him. One must assume that this was a reciprocal arrangement: either the herder offers one goat to the god, who in return assures the safety of the rest of the flock, especially from wolves (Stroszeck 2002);[63] or, contrariwise, the herdsman offers the goat as a thanks offering for the previous safekeeping vouchsafed by the god (much along the lines of later votive offerings).

It would seem that in its origins, the cult of Pan was diffuse in locus; that is, it was assumed that he needed no special cave, grove or building. He inhabited the mountaintop, the mountain, the region: it was all sacred to him.

While temples and built structures were not unknown in his cult (Borgeaud 1988), it was far more common for people to worship him in caves, in rock formations or cracks in rocks (Stroszeck 2002); even in Athens, rather than erect a temple for him, the citizens came to find him in a fissure in the stone, which had been dedicated to him. I would suggest that this is not to say that Pan refuses to enter buildings or is not at home in them: rather, that those who wish to interact with him find it easier to do so in surroundings which hark back to the wilderness from which the god comes. This is not to eschew the workings of humans: after all, the offerings are often things that are made by humans (cakes, cheese, meat which has been dressed), and indeed, humans are there to make the offerings themselves.

Having begun among shepherds and in the wild mountains, Pan and his cult made the trek from the countryside to the city, after (if not before) the battle of Marathon (Haldane 1968; Borgeaud 1988; Lonsdale

---

[63] It would be fascinating, though outside the scope of the present work, to muse upon the coincidence (if such it is) that Pan and the werewolf originate from one small area of Greece – the half man, half animal god, and the man who becomes an animal (for a space of years, rather than at the turn of the moon, in the ancient Greek tale).

1993; Stroszeck 2002). Herodotus, among others (Nonnus; Pausanias), tells the story:

> While [the Athenians were] still in the city [at the start of the Persian War], the generals first sent to Sparta the herald Philippides, an Athenian and a long-distance runner who made that his calling. As Philippides himself said when he brought the message to the Athenians, when he was in the Parthenian mountain above Tegea he encountered Pan. Pan called out Philippides' name and bade him ask the Athenians why they paid him no attention, though he was of goodwill to the Athenians, had often been of service to them, and would be in the future. The Athenians believed that these things were true, and when they became prosperous they established a sacred precinct of Pan beneath the Akropolis. Ever since that message they propitiate him with annual sacrifices and a torch-race. (Herodotus, 6. 105)

There is much that could be said (and has been[64]) about this passage. Perhaps the most interesting thing to strike the reader is that Philippides immediately recognises Pan – even though from the story, it is clear that his worship had not yet been established in Athens. One might suggest that, as a long-distance messenger by trade (he had "made that his calling"), Philippides might well have come across Pan's cult in some other city, or have passed by some roadside shrine (although this last is unlikely, as Pan seems to have been worshipped in places more inaccessible than not (Pausanias; Borgeaud 1988)). Or perhaps the concept of Pan was known before his formal worship was accepted in the city – certainly some of the fragments we have about Pan predate the Persian war. And, when you get right down to it, the god does have a rather striking appearance.

It is also interesting that Pan does not need to ask Philippides his nationality, as it were – Pan seems to know that Philippides hails from

---

[64] (Allen 1904; Harrison 1926; Haldane 1968; Hammond 1968; Hillman and Roscher 1972; Stillwell, MacDonald et al. 1976; Borgeaud 1988; Larson 2001; Stroszeck 2002; Clauss 2003; Wilson 2004)

Athens, and reminds him of the services the god has rendered to the city state.

Perhaps most interesting, however, is the ready acceptance by the citizens of Athens that Pan had, indeed, come to their aid, and should be accorded the honour of an annual sacrifice and indeed a place on the acropolis. Neither Pan (in the story) nor Herodotus (in the retelling) enlightens us as to what the services provided by the god were; we must, however, assume that the good men of Athens picked up on the not overly subtle hint[65] and acted on it.

Slightly less obvious but nonetheless important is the quid pro quo nature of ancient Greek worship highlighted by this passage. Why should the people of Athens honour Pan? Because he has done good things for them in the past (and surely the fact that the runner is involved in carrying news about a war may give a hint as to the locus of those good things?). There is no wounded pride on the part of the goat foot god; he does not demand worship on the basis of his standing as a god, or his virtue, or even his virility; rather, he merely asks for that which is due to him.

There is no threat to his words, no statement of what might happen should his plea be disregarded. However, the Athenians knew their lore as well as anyone else: those who go against the wishes of this god (as against the wishes of most of the gods, to be truthful) find themselves mad, at best, and torn limb from limb at worst. In that sort of situation, even without a clear threat, non-compliance takes a great deal more bravery (and foolhardiness) than might otherwise be the case.

But even within the worship of the god himself, we find echoes of his special talents: places which were sacred to him seem to have been associated with possession (Borgeaud 1988). Pan was not to be approached in silence, as were other gods – rather, women came him singing and laughing[66] (Menander), with a "just excess."

---

[65] This is, after all, Pan – not a deity known for subtlety...

[66] This may be a family trait, as it seems that it was Pan's daughter, Iambe, who caused Demeter to cease mourning for Kore and laugh (Apollodorus 1999).

This relates, again, to what we have already seen about the goat foot god: although he is linked with sex, he is not often related to marriage (although he is at times associated with goddesses who are), yet he is more than merely tolerated in a society which prized legitimacy above so much else. His excesses – and they *are* excesses, when one considers how often the outcome of his attentions was not favourable to the recipient – are accorded a place in ancient Greek society. It would seem that his actions are accepted (perhaps they provide an outlet, for the constrained and contained ancient Greek?). It is also worth noting, perhaps, that we find that in some stories at least, the main celebrants of his rites are women – and that in general, his rites begin with the ideas and work of one individual, who draws others along with them. The cult seems to have been, for the most part at least, one of individual and personal devotion (Borgeaud 1988). Although he offers his protection – or something – to Athens, he remains mainly a god honoured by individuals, who relates to people one on one, people who come to honour him, ask him for boons, and leave offerings.

And what were those offerings? They may be divided into two simple classes: the physical (which were in the main the usual sorts of things) and the non-physical (which is where the cult of Pan becomes in some ways unique – or at least unusual).

Animals offered to Pan matched the god himself: male, and uncastrated.[67] However, it was not unusual to find more simple offerings: cakes, cheese, bread; these were offered to the nymphs as well as to Pan (Borgeaud 1988). Of course, that makes sense – Pan is, after all, the god of the countryside, rather than the prosperous city (even within the city, he retains the flavour of the country). Merivale quotes an offering script:

> Charicles by the wooded hill offered to Pan who loves the rock
> this yellow bearded goat, a horned creature to the horned, a
> hairy one to the hairy-legged, a bounding one to the deft

---

[67] Tortoises were also thought to be sacred to Pan, at least on Mt. Parthenius, (Pausanias, 8.54.7).

leaper, a denizen of the woods to the forest god. (Merivale 1991)[68]

There are also votive offerings: figurines depicting Pan and/or the nymphs (with whom he was so frequently associated, see below), golden cicadas, pots, etc. (Borgeaud 1988).

In terms of the nonmaterial offerings, there is a particular cry, brought forth by women and called "krauge," which forms a part of panic ritual, as well as the "laughter and a just excess" proper to the worship of Pan (Borgeaud 1988). That final phrase may sum up a great deal about the goat foot god *and* his place in classical Greece.

As we have seen, life in classical Greece, particularly classical Athens, was controlled by laws, social norms and mores, by the expectations of a host of different groups and individuals: much like life in almost any other society. The relationships between the sexes were (in theory)[69] highly regulated, cf. Demosthenes' famous delineation of the classes of women (Demosthenes). Yet this same society found room within it not only for the worship of Pan, but for that of Dionysos – both of which included ecstatic rites *for women.* [70] Women out of control were to be feared, but they were also to be sanctioned: in their proper place and time.

And so it is for the worship of Pan: it includes a "just excess" – a breaking of the boundaries, a routing of the law is allowed, *in that space and time, by those particular people.* Wine (allowed for Pan but never for the nymphs), sexual excess, dreams and possession can all be part of any relationship with Pan. His worship combined music and inarticulate cries; careful dances and panic movements – he embodies the tensions within classical society.

---

[68] Note how the image of the god seen above in relation to the Hymn is reinforced by the belief inherent in the cult.

[69] One suspects, however, that the lived reality was as messy for the Greeks as it is for the rest of humanity...

[70] For the significance of this, see: (Diotima 2004)

Pan walks this sort of fine line between his fellow divinities, as well as between the order and (threatened) chaos of human relations. Attempts to delineate the place of the goat foot god in relation to other gods are doomed to fail, in the face of conflicting information and representation. We have seen above that there is no agreement even in terms of his parentage: is he the son of Hermes, or the foster brother of Zeus (which would lend a nicely goat-y feel), or is there some other explanation for him?

Pan appears as auxiliary or adjunct to a wide variety of gods: the nymphs, of course, but also Dionysos, the Great Mother, (he is styled as the "dog of the Great Mother" by Pindar) Aphrodite and even Artemis and Demeter, the very goddesses one might expect to find most opposed to all that Pan represents: the virgin goddess and the protector of the hearth. Yet it is Pan who finds Demeter as she wanders the world in her grief for the missing Kore (Pausanias, 8. 42. 1). Pan finds her because he (alone of the gods?) can enter where she sits, a place devoid of cult, sterile, barren. Boregaud suggests that Pan functions here as a mediator between the Olympians and the mourning mother (Borgeaud 1988).

Perhaps this may function as a suitable end to this chapter on the cult of Pan, as it shows the flexible, voluble, variable nature of the goat god so well. Demeter is nothing if not domesticated – she is, in many ways, not just symbolic of the hearth but is the hearth, the heart of the home, itself. And yet, it is Pan alone of all the gods – the one who is ever welcome and never settled on Olympus – he who dances alongside the majestic stride of Dionysos and the capering of his father Hermes – he who is both lord of the hunt and the hound of the Goddess – who can find Demeter when all others cannot see her; it is Pan, ever liminal, who can draw her back from her mourning, and recall her to the duties she carries and the care she must have for all of humanity.

And all the while, he plays on the syrinx, chases the nymphs, and eludes exact definition. I suspect that would please him...

Dancing god
      Laughing god
            You who make armies flee

Goat footed god
      Hermes' son
            Will you dance with me?

Within the city scape you find me
      No daughter of the land
The daily grind entwines and binds me
      Will you offer me your hand?

Even in the city streets
      There's wilderness to find
Among the stone and marble seats
      Of learning and of mind

For Arcadia's a state of mind
      As well as forest dim
If I look for you, will I find
      You dancing, there, within....?

Dancing god
      Laughing god
            Terror brought at noon

Laughing god
      Dangerous god
            Will you dance with me .... soon?

("Dancing God" Diotima 2004; 2005)

While it would be possible to trace the footprints – hoof prints? – of Pan throughout the ages since the demise of classical Greece, that has been done elsewhere and is outside our sphere of interest here (those who wish to read on this subject are advised to begin with Merivale's work (Merivale 1969), and go from there). Rather, here we are interested in what is made of Pan by the "modern scene" – what is likely to be understood about, said about or written about Pan, today?

So, what has Pan become in the modern, New Age scene?

Remarkably muddled, is what he's become – or at least perceptions of him have become so.

Take, as a fairly classic example, the song, "Lord of the Flame,"

> He is Osiris, and he is also Pan
> And he is god, but he is also man
> (Inkubus Sukkubus)

Pardon?

While it is true to say that Herodotus did make a connection between Pan and certain Egyptian deities, I am unaware of any ancient source that confuses Osiris (Lord of the *Dead*) with Pan (who, as we have seen, is quintessentially the lord of living things). It is far more likely that Pan is aligned to Mendes, or the ram headed god Khum, than to Osiris, if there is any connection in his background to Egypt at all. (And the connection to Khum would only be a visual one – and it's the wrong half of the goat, anyway.)

The story of Osiris is well enough known.[71] The brother/husband of Isis, his role in the main myth concerning him is to be killed by his brother Seth, and then to magically impregnate Isis. Even when resurrected, he rules over the dead, and is generally seen as having black skin (that being the colour of life for the ancient Egyptians, who depended so heavily on the Nile flood soil for their existence).

---

[71] If it is not, have a look in, among others: (Griffiths 1955; Waterson 1996; Geddes and Grosset 1997; Bennett and Crowley 2001; David 2002; Sykes and Kendall 2002; Fletcher 2003).

So, confusion the first – since when is Pan (lord of living creatures) the same as Osiris (lord of the dead)?

As for "He is god but he is also man." It's true that there is one ancient reference to Pan as a man who became a god, but that is one reference among, as we have seen, many hundreds – and there are few, if any, such references for Osiris. Neither of them is generally reckoned to belong to that race of heroes who become deities at death (or instead of dying). It is true that early sources speak of the constellation of Capricorn as being in honour of Pan but even in these, it is clearly a deity being commemorated. While it is more than possible to find man to god correspondences in the ancient world, the motif does not apply here; and in fact, the far more likely source for this phrase and concept is the pervasive Christian idea of the incarnation and kenosis (emptying of self) – not an archetype of either Pan or Osiris, really, but of the two closer to Osiris.

If we move back a bit in the song, we find:

Angel of Light, and Lord of the Sacred Flame
A liberator to free you from your shame
Ride out and set the slaves all free
Fill our souls with your love and with your ecstasy

Angel(?) of love (?!) – Pan?

Again, it must be admitted that the general impression given of angels bears little, if any, resemblance to their depiction in ancient sources (Davidson 1967; Diotima 2006; Diotima 2006), it is also true that few of the ancient sources about them can be made to fit into any even remotely Pan-like mode.

And, again, it is true that one might see both Pan and Osiris in terms of liberators – but neither of them function to release people from their "shame" (again, an overtly Christian idea, along with the freeing of people from slavery). Pan frees Psyche (or allows her to free herself) from the desire to kill herself; he might be said to free people from restraint (cf. the requirement not to approach him silently but to do so making a great noise). Panic might be said to be a release of a (generally unwelcome) type, while the healing side of Pan might be seen as a liberator.

All of which is a large stretch and not in any way related to what we have seen about Pan's perception in the past.

"Lord of the sacred flame" – this, at last, has some resonance; as we have seen, Pan was honoured by a torch race, and a fire was kept ever kindled in his sanctuaries. So that one, at least, might have some basis in the idea/l of Pan.

One out of... how many?

While it may seem unfair to concentrate on an admittedly popular (as opposed to scholarly) source such as an I.S. song, the truth is that many modern/postmodern representations of Pan fall into many of the same traps. Over just the period of the preparation of this book, I have seen Pan equated to or with: the Green Man (who may well be as much Christian as Pagan (Basford 2004)), Osiris as above, Loki, Coyote (on the grounds of being a "trickster" – though I've never been able to figure out how Pan is such), and of course in these islands the perennial favourite, Cernunnos.

Cernunnos himself is a bit of an enigma for scholars: after all, he's only named the once, and that on an altar raised by sailors in France (Green 1992; Green 2004). Or, perhaps it would be more accurate to say he is described – because of course Cernunnos is no more a proper name – or was no more a proper name, anyway, than "shorty" or "big ears" – it means "horned one." Yet, so many of the representations we have of him, or that are ascribed to him, have not horns but antlers – the difference between permanent horns and antlers, which are shed with the seasons, should be clear, as should the associations of each. It is hard to see how they could be the same.

But over and over again, one comes across the idea that all horned (or indeed, antlered) gods are the same god, with the same attributes. While this might be a possible explanation, it is difficult to see how such disparate deities might come together under one heading: particularly when the attributes of one simply don't fit with the others. The Horned God is often seen as the personification of the young and vital: yet almost all ancient depictions of Pan show a man not of young years but in vital middle age;[72] the Horned God is seen as a psychopomp, the one thing we have seen is never attributed to Pan. (Perhaps his father, with his interesting cap and sandals, might fulfil the role?)

The connection with Loki, which one hears with increasing frequency, is even more baffling. While there are some similarities, they are few...

First of all, Loki is a giant – the son and father of giants, and generally of giant stock – and, as we've seen, Pan is anything but, being shown more often than not as shorter than average men. Loki is best known for his cunning, by means of which he more than once gets his fellow residents of Asgard out of, if not hot water (all things considered), then difficult situations. It is by his trickery that the Aesir are absolved from paying for the building of the walls around their home, for instance.

Pan, as we've seen, provides help to the Olympians in their struggle against the Titans. Loki accomplishes his feat by shape shifting (becoming a mare); Pan may well have changed shape during the struggle with the Titans (hence the shape of the constellation related to him).

Further, Loki is responsible for various acquisitions by the Aesir: Thor's hammer, the recovery of Idun's apples (and Idun herself), etc. As we have seen, Pan gifted the world with the Pan pipes and perhaps the art of prophecy.

There, as far as I can see, the links between the two end. There is no record so far as I know of Pan deceiving anyone or outwitting anyone. In the later tales at least, Loki ends up reviled by the Aesir, chained to a rock by the entrails of his son, suffering from the poison dripping on him from the snake above.

Pan, on the other hand, "delighted all the gods" at his birth and there is no record that this delight ever waned. The connection between the two simply does not stand up, in any substantial way.

---

[72] While it is true that "middle age" for the ancient Greeks would have been attained at an age we would still consider young – mid 20s to early 30s at most – that's not the point; the contemporary depictions of Pan are not of a young man or young deity; they are of a man in full years and full prowess.

This excursus (perhaps "diatribe" might be more accurate) is not meant to deny the value of any UPG (unsubstantiated personal gnosis) experienced by an individual. There is no authority over such things and each person must make of her own experiences what she will; as mentioned above, there is no real need to give any more weight to the stories of the ancients than those of our own day, at least not simply on the grounds of age alone.

However, the question becomes, when is a goat not a goat? How far does the conception of a god have to move from the original conception, before we are no longer talking about the same deity?

I suspect that the interesting interpretations of Pan given above are due more to a lamentable lack of accuracy[73] than to changed perceptions of the god.

However, this lacks any positive contribution on my part – how do I see Pan, in the modern day?

First, I would say that others have answered this question before I, and done so well (even if I do not always agree with their conclusions). I would recommend Robbins' *Jitterbug Perfume* (Robbins 2001) as a case in point.[74]

It is also worth pointing out that most of our views of Pan from the ancient lore, indeed, most of those presented here, are from myths and plays, as well as relics, rather than from scholarly tomes: what we know most about is what people believed, rather than what the academics felt they *should* believe (which is, I think, always a good thing). Thus, I have already suggested a novel as a means of accessing the idea of Pan in the modern day.

I would further take the initiative and suggest that other fiction and poetry could support modern views of Pan – such as those found in *Refuge* (Diotima 2005), as well as what often amount to cameo

---

[73] This is a polite way of saying, "sloppy work."

[74] And, indeed, a case in point of how I would not agree with the author's conclusion. I have no wish to ruin the book for anyone who has not read it, so I will only say that the picture painted of Pan in the modern day in *Jitterbug Perfume* is depressing, at best.

appearances made by the god in places such as Gaiman's novel (Gaiman 2005).

Otherwise... how does Pan fit into life in the 21st Century?

The obvious answer to that is: however he wishes to do. However, the obvious is not always the most helpful...

I suspect he will fit into this century as he fit into all the others: in his own inimitable style. If we look at the attributes we've ascribed to him through the ancient sources, perhaps we can more clearly see his place in our own time.

First and foremost, Pan represents an out-of-bounds sexuality; he is the wild, he is the unconventional. I hesitate to say where Pan would be found on a typical Saturday night in, say, London or New York... as much as anything because I suspect that the answer would be different for each individual.

Because what Pan represents is not *just* the unconventional: he represents what is challenging *for the individual concerned*. For those who have never stepped aside from the usual and the expected, he would be the unusual and that which would be surprising. For those who already walk what might be called a knife edge of innovation, perhaps he would represent the opposite?

Then again, Pan is a hunter. While it would be politically correct to point out that he was so at a time when those who hunted were providing for the table, and didn't hunt for sport, this assertion is difficult to uphold: although the spoil of the hunt almost certainly was either eaten or offered, it's clear from some of the passages cited above that people hunted for sport as well as for provision – even if they ate the proceeds, they enjoyed the game. There's no suggestion in any of the ancient texts that Pan would approve of hunting only for consumption – however, it must be admitted that there is no answer to this dichotomy simply because the question would not have arisen. I don't think there's any way, on the basis of the ancient texts, to elicit Pan's support for either the pro- or anti-hunting lobby – the debate is framed in categories which would have made no sense to the ancients.

However, it is perhaps significant that when we see Pan hunting, he is doing so with his own hands – he *runs* after his prey; he uses a staff, spear or rudimentary slingshot to bring down the game. While this doesn't rule out his patronage of hunting with more modern weapons, one is tempted to say that the more risk and energy needed on the part of the hunter, the closer the exercise is to that for which Pan is seen as patron.

What are we to make of Panic, in the modern context? There is plenty of panic around today – but I suspect this is far too simplistic a solution.

What Panic, properly speaking, represents is instability, but not just any old garden or common variety instability – I think there is little precedent for seeing Pan as an anarchist, for instance.[75] Rather, Pan's panic is that provided for his friends, for those "on his side" – quite literally, he provides "confusion to our enemies." He's not about spreading random panic or confusion; he is very targeted in what he does.

In light of the current world situation, I think it also worth noting that laughter is a particular attribute of the goat-god; he is seen laughing, laughter is seen as his gift or a sign of his presence, or even as a sign of being possessed by him. Nowhere is it recorded that this laughter is at the expense of another – rather, it seems to be the laughter born of the pure joy of existence, the laughter engendered by exercise, by the dance, by music, by companionship.

I hesitate to offer suggestions, firstly because everyone's solutions will be unique to themselves – if the Pan archetype teaches us nothing else, it teaches us the value of the individual. Secondly, because I have no desire to be blamed for decisions taken by others. It is, however, perhaps significant that the city fathers of Athens never sought to ban the worship of Pan, as being dangerous to the state – while they did ban the worship of other deities on that basis.

---

[75] Certainly not as a card-carrying anarchist, which must in itself be some sort of contradiction in terms.

Pan and the feminist consciousness

Not a spurned lover, but a rapist – can a feminist be involved with, interested in Pan? Feel free to skip this section, if the question has no resonance for you. For me, however, it is an issue which has required thought and adjustment over the course of some years...

Before one can begin any discussion with as exalted a title as this chapter, one must define terms. And, perhaps oddly, the first term in such need of definition is the name of the god himself – or, to put it more clearly – which concept of Pan is to be used in this discussion?

It will come as no surprise to readers who have persevered this far that my own preference is for the ancient understandings of the god, rather than the more sedate and indeed all but saccharine (and vanilla) descriptions one tends to find in rather more modern works. We have seen the transformation undergone by the concept of Pan since the fateful call to Tamuz. It would be a mammoth undertaking to relate each of these images to any concept of feminist theory and/or feminism; I trust that I may be forgiven then for concentrating on the ancient (and indeed, far more coherent, for some value of that term) views. "Pan," then, will be defined in this discussion as he appears in the earliest chapters of this book.

That's the easy part.

Defining feminism, or the feminist consciousness, hasn't been easy since the word was first used in English at the end of the nineteenth century – and indeed, the general concept has been in dispute for much longer than that. Definitions range from the simple, that women are full human beings with all this entails (Cleage 1993), to the more radical representations of feminism to be found from Daly (Daly 1973) to Solanis (Solanis). There is no agreement among feminists, particularly among academic feminists, as to what feminism is,[76] and I have no intention of entering the lists of definition by offering any new or honoured definition – hence the title of this chapter is "Pan and the feminist consciousness" rather than "Pan and feminism" per se...

Rather, I shall adopt a middle line between the radical, essentialist views (all women share one burden, all men are equivalent in their oppressive practices) and the stance which focuses almost entirely on obtaining change through legal sanction. As with most people who go through the processes of committing words to paper and the parturition process that is bringing a book to birth, I firmly believe in the power of language to shape thought and behaviour, but do not subscribe to the universalist idea(l) that all women are oppressed by an inherent patriarchy.

Rather, "the feminist consciousness" here will be understood as a stance for critique, rather than a political platform: one might cogently speak of the lens of feminism, as a vehicle through which to view the goat foot god, his mythos and story.

Understood in this way, the feminist lens would be a concentration of a series of concepts and viewpoints. It would search for and highlight the presence or absence of the female voice (with all of the attendant issues brought about by applying such a lens to what is in the main a body of literature with its origins in oral retellings). It would foreground the experience of women (females – in the case of Pan, this would include goddesses, human females and perhaps the odd goat).

Such a lens would also take into account the society at which it was trained: the mythos of the goat foot god arises in a particular time and place. No man is an island and even gods are contextual.

One thing this lens will not do, however, is put Pan in some sort of loco homo – that is, he will not be assumed to stand for all men nor will he be seen as some sort of representative of masculinity. He is, as we have seen above, rather impossible to box in, and this particular set of boxes fits him no better than any other.

---

[76] It is not surprising, but continues to be depressing, that there is far more agreement among those who disparage feminism, as to what it might be, than those who work to further what they perceive to be its aims.

This is not the place for an in-depth review of gender issues in ancient Greece – this topic has seen lively discussion for a good number of years and information is readily available (McClure; O'Faolain and Martines 1973; Gould 1980; Keuls 1985; Alic 1986; Lefkowitz 1986; Kleinberg 1988; Cohen 1989; Ehernberg 1989; Schaps 1989; Duby and Perrot 1990; Georgoudi 1990; Loraux 1990; Pantel 1990; Rousselle 1990; Scheid 1990; Sissa 1990; Thomas 1990; Zaidman 1990, among many, many others; Duby&Perrot 1992; Katz 1992; Laquer 1992; Lefkowitz and Fant 1992; Bullough 1993; Brock 1994; Maurizio 1995; Beard and Henderson 1997; Thornton 1997; Anderson and Zissner 1999; Metraux 1999; David 2000; Voss 2000; Pratt 2000 ; Larson 2001; Johnstone 2003; Lyons 2003). A fairly superficial review of the essential elements is all that is needed here.

The Greece of Pan (that is, the various states which come under the general heading of "ancient Greece") was for the most part a patriarchal society. This does not mean (merely) that "men were in charge." Literally, it means "rule by the father" and most if not all of these societies were prime examples of what might be called a "proper patriarchy" – in general, the eldest male of a family group had almost total power over everyone else in the group – other men as well as women.[77]

Axiomatically, "the glory of an Athenian woman is to be spoken of in neither praise nor blame," which is often taken as a de facto statement of the total lack of voice allotted to women in that society. And, from the point of view of the 21st century, there are any number of practices which rather confirm this – marriage of girls of 15 to men twice their age, whom they had quite possibly never met, in a ceremony that more or less ritualised rape and abduction; separate spheres of activity for men and women in the home, lack of civil and legal rights, institutionalised slavery and prostitution, not to mention the famous delineation between wives for legitimate offspring, mistresses for bodily needs, and hetaerae (high class prostitutes) for pleasure

---

[77] It is instructive to realise that there *is* no word in classical Greek for "family" meaning group of related humans. Rather, the closest word includes not only people but property.

(Demosthenes). Women were, no matter what their age, always viewed as legal minors in Athens (Gould 1980). Keuls, in a work which is dated but still of interest, waxes eloquent about the significance of the motif of "the killing of the Amazon" as central to the Athenian self-definition (Keuls 1985).

However, we must be clear about our context. As I have argued elsewhere, it seems that the societies of ancient Greece certainly sought to control women, on the grounds that in doing so, they assured the smooth sailing of society as a whole – in other words, the thing about women is (was) not that they were power*less* but that, unbridled, they would be too power*ful* – which is dangerous (Diotima 2004). Women who were out of place (Amazons) or out of control (Agave, when maddened by the god, or Antigone, when she chose to follow the dictates of the gods rather than the state, embodied in her uncle[78]). The reason for this is quite simple: unregulated women are antithetical to a kin based society which relies on descent through the paternal line. Seen in this light, practices become more coherent and understandable (if in no way excusable).

So what, then, of Pan in this society, through this feminist lens?

The first issue might be that of the female voice. Where, in the mythos of Pan, do we hear the words of women?

And immediately we are presented with the paradox that is Echo, whose voice is often heard but whose words are (almost never) her own. Echo could well stand as a symbol of the ancient Greek view of woman: disembodied, placeless, never speaking of her own accord, and giving back only a pale, muted imitation of what is spoken to her. Her very being is one of weakness and reaction rather than strength and purposeful, chosen activity.

---

[78] Is it at all significant that Antigone's punishment – living burial – was the same as that allotted to Roman Vestals who were found not to be virgins? The crime, after all, was essentially the same – treason. And the reason for the particular punishment – which killed without bloodshed or violence – the same. Violence against a Vestal was unthinkable, and Creon already had more than enough kin blood to answer for without adding that of a virgin niece.

And she gets into this state... due to the unbridled lust of the goat foot god.

Even a cursory reading of the tales of Echo, Pitys and Syrinx makes it fairly clear that Pan (in spite of the way he is at times depicted by romantic and indeed, Romantic writers) is no lovelorn suitor, pining due to polite rejection. In blunt terms, he is a frustrated rapist.

This may sound harsh but it does also appear to be the truth.

Pitys, Echo, Syrinx – these nymphs ran from Pan in mortal fear (and, in Pitys' case, to some extent fear of the immortals, as her virginity was vowed to the goddess[79]). While Pan is portrayed as wooing Selene (and even then using deception to attain his goal), it would seem that what he was attempting to use in the case of the nymphs would very accurately be named brute force.

(Although it is interesting to note that the goat foot god, whom we have seen heralded as fleet of foot, swift at the hunt, and so on, seems perpetually unable to catch the nymphs in time. Syrinx stops not because Pan has caught her, but because she has come to the water's edge. Pitys might have been caught eventually, but there is time for her transformation to take place before Pan reaches her. This god who could easily hunt, chase and catch the lynx and hare seems to have been singularly unable to outrun young females – even though he is always seen as a powerful man at or just barely past his prime. I surmise nothing in particular from this, but merely raise it as a point for attention.)

That same brute force supervises (in at least one telling of the story) the most horrific encounter with a female in the corpus of ancient tales about Pan. Echo is, for her crime of rejecting the love of men, dismembered as the god looks on, and her "still singing" limbs strewn about the world.

While this is clearly a tale told to explain the origin of the echo phenomenon, it must at least have made sense to those who told and

---

[79] While we today might well say that a woman raped has in no way violated such a vow, and while we might even find support in such ancient authorities as Augustine (The City of God), not all societies would – or do – share that understanding.

retold the tale – as the functionalists remind us, nothing remains long in a society if it does not fulfil a function for that society. If no one could conceive of Pan being angry enough, or brutal enough, to watch the killing of the nymph, surely the tale would not have survived?

I have called Echo a paradox – and so she is. For while her death – at the behest and under the gaze of Pan – is recorded by one author, in the story of Psyche, Echo is seen "reclining in the arms of Pan." That there is such a contradiction in the lore should not surprise us by this point, but it does serve to demonstrate that Pan is much more than a simple herdsman.

It has to be said that this tale is an unusual one. As we've seen above, Pan is much more likely to be hunting (game or sexual partners) or causing panic and disturbance, than he is to be seen dispensing really quite sensible advice to suicidal young women. The passage seems more linked to the images of Pan as a warrior above – but even these show him engaged in battle at one remove – causing panic, rather than wielding a battle axe. And even in the tales of the death of Echo, he stands and watches, rather than participates directly.

So – what is a feminist to make of Pan?

Can a feminist have any sort of relationship with or to the goat foot god, and retain any integrity at all *as* a feminist?

I don't intend to suggest an answer to these questions – they are queries each must answer for herself.

But I will suggest some ways forward...

The first is one that I admit at the outset is probably specious, is definitely dubious and may be simply silly – but should carry a caveat as possibly dangerous. It is to suggest that interactions with feminists might have a rehabilitating effect on Pan; that perhaps by hearing, seeing and knowing how the world has changed, the god himself may change.

(But does he *need* to change? Perhaps to satisfy the dictates of feminism, he need only remember and emulate his interactions with Psyche rather more than any others?)

The second is perhaps more workable – it certainly has more integrity. And it is to admit that not everything in the world is neat, tidy and easily pigeonholed – that not everything surrounding a feminist can

82

accord with her[80] particular philosophy. This is not meant to be a panacea (no pun intended) nor does it remove from the feminist any possible conflict of interest. It is merely an acknowledgement that the world is not as simple or as easy as it might be.

---

[80] The careful reader will have seen that I've used "her" throughout, in place of the "generic he;" I use it here to be consistent, rather than to suggest that all feminists must be female – an argument I have no intention of joining here.

Not an end so much as a pause....

So, where does this leave us, with our study of Pan?

In many ways, right where we began. We know perhaps more, we have pondered a bit more deeply – we have seen the god of the hunt meld with the god who brings fear in war and riot in sex – we see Hermes' son and Dionysos' companion...

I would at this juncture like to return to some of the earliest musings in this work, those surrounding mythos and logos.

Like it or not, we are firmly people of the logos; our upbringing, our society, our education, our press and media: all incline us to prize the rational over the emotional (and yes, the male over the female because of associations made between the genders and those two poles of existence).

Most of what we have seen of Pan dates from not the absolute time of mythos, nor yet is it embedded in our world of logos. Rather, it dates from that period in history which was neither the one nor the other: the time when the philosophers were debating truth at the same time as their contemporaries were filling graveyards with little leaden scrolls and dolls to accomplish their wills by magic (Frankfurter 1995; Gordon 1999; Ogden 1999; Faraone 2004); when the loftiest ideals of the academy and the theatre lived cheek by jowl with infanticide, slavery and warfare for conquest... A time, indeed, which may truly be called liminal. A few hundred years either way, and one is either mythos-oriented or logos-oriented, at least in the West.

And in the centre – we find Pan.

How very, very apt – for he is, if nothing else, quintessentially liminal. Arcadia is his homeland, neither forest nor plain, but rather mountains and scrub. Even when he is in Athens, he is honoured as no other god; no temple is raised to him but he finds a home in a natural feature in a human-raised city.

And as Merivale has so aptly shown (Merivale 1969), he never really leaves the western mind. For good or ill, whether it is his death we hear proclaimed or a hedgehog we find nestling between his hooves (Grahame 1917), whether he drives women to madness and death

85

(Machen 1894) or somehow restores the pride of an English village (Dunsany 2003) or even provides the solution to an olfactory conundrum (Robbins 2001), whether invoked by mages (Crowley 1919) or repudiated by clerics who see him as akin to the devil, he seems to have retained our fascination in a way many other deities have not.

I suspect he is remarkably amused about that....

Lament at Banias

They come to see
       The touch of the god
              Beside the cave and fire
They bring their gifts
       Of sacrifice
              They bring their staid desires

"A working hand" "A mended back"
       "My legs be strong and true"
And these I grant
       But more, I crave
           The few...

Who know the cost
       And count it dear
But balk not at the price

For what I would heal
       Is humanity

Come – let me show you – life

A life well-lived
       In joy and pain
       Throw off the binding chains

Throw off the rules
       Throw off the thoughts
       Till only – you – remain

Be mad with me
       And dance, and leap

By Panic, be you found
The goat-foot god
  The healing god
  Pipes a maenad sound

Be healed
  If you will
  If that will satisfy

But for those of you
  Fore those fair few
  Who grasp the wings to fly

Seek healing not
  But brokenness
  And Panic – pain, and strife
For only then
  And only so
    Will you understand this life

Saltless meat
  Is thin, sour wine
  The spice, is food indeed
Come dance with me
  Says the goat foot god
  As he plays upon the reed

The great god Pan they called me then
  And feared, themselves, to be...

There are few who may
  Fewer still, who will

Now come – will you – dance with me?

(Diotima 2005)

Appendix 1: The Homeric Hymn to Pan (XIX)

Muse,
speak to me of the loved child
of Hermes

with his goat's feet
and his two horns

the one who loves noise

who roams about
in wooded meadows
together with
dancing nymphs who tread upon

peaks of rock
even goats leave bare
calling out

Pan

god of shepherds
dust-parched
with dazzling hair

who has
all the snowy crests
and the mountain ridges
and the rocky paths
for his home.

Here and there
he roams
through dense thickets

and sometimes
he is drawn
to soft streams
and sometimes
he wanders back
over precipices of rock
climbing
up to the
highest peak
to watch over his sheep.

Often he runs along
shining distant mountains
and often
he races down
the mountain sides
killing wild beasts,
so piercing is his eye.

Only in the evening
when he lets go the hunt
then he makes sounds
on his pipes of reed
playing a sweet deep song.

and no bird
can surpass him
in song

not even she who
when spring is full of flowers
pours fourth her lament
among the leaves
singing with honey voice
a mournful song.

Then the clear-singing
mountain nymphs
roam around with him
on their strong feet
chanting by a spring
of clear water

while Echo
on the mountain-top
wails.

The god

now this
side of the chorus
now that

or at times
gliding
into the midst of them

conducts the dancing feet

wearing the blood-red
skin of a lynx
upon his back

his heart
delighting in
the shrill songs
in a soft meadow
where crocuses
and sweet-smelling hyacinths
mix in with the grass
wherever they like.

They sing of the blessed gods
and high Olympos
they tell of Hermes
who brings luck
beyond all others
how he is the swift messenger
of all the gods

and how he came to Arcadia
with its many springs
mother of the flocks
where Kyllene is
the sacred place
of the god.

And there
though he was a god
he tended the sheep
with their shaggy fleece
for a mortal man

all because

there came over him
and intensified

melting longing

to lie with
the nymph with the beautiful hair,
daughter of Dryops.

It ended in joyous marriage.

And in the house she gave birth
to a dear son for Hermes

who from the first
was marvellous to look upon

with goat's feet
and two horns,
loving noise
and laughing sweetly.

But his mother jumped up
and ran away.

As soon as she
caught sight of
his harsh face
and this thick beard
she was terrified
and left the child alone.

Quickly Hermes
who brings the luck
took him in his arms
accepting him

and happy in his heart
beyond measure
was the god.

So quickly
wrapping his son
in the warm skins
of mountain hares

he went to the home
of the immortal gods
and he sat down
beside Zeus and the other gods

and showed them his boy.

Then all the immortal gods
were glad in their hearts
but most of all
Bacchos Dionysos.

They called him

Pan

because he delighted
the hearts
of all.

And so to you lord
farewell
I would please you
with my song.

And now I shall remember you
And another song too.

(Richardson 2003, pp. 119, ff)

Greek Lyric V Anonymous, Fragments 936 *(Inscription from the shrine of Asclepius at Epidaurus.*

Hymn to Hermes. London, Penguin Books.

Aeschylus. "Eumenides " Translated by: Herbert Weir Smyth, Ph. D., Ed. Retrieved 4.6.06.

Aeschylus "Persians."

Alic, M. (1986). *Hypatia's Heritage.* London, The Women's Press.

Allen, T. W. (1897). "The text of the Homeric Hymns, III." *The Journal of Hellenic Studies* **17**: 42 - 62.

Allen, T. W. (1904). "Commentary on the Homeric Hymns." Retrieved 2.6.06, from http://www.chlt.org/sandbox/perseus/allen.hh_eng/page.o.a.php.

Anderson, B. S. and J. P. Zissner (1999). *A history of their own: Women in Europe from prehistory to the present.* Oxford, Oxford University Press.

Apollodorus (1999). *The Library of Greek Mythology.* Oxford, Oxford University Press.

Apollonius Rhodius *Argonautica.*

Apuleius (1999). The Golden Ass. Oxford, Oxford Paperbacks.

Aristophanes. (1938). "Women at the Thesmophoria." Translator: Eugene O'Neill. Retrieved 4.6.06.

Aristotle *The Politics.*

Armstrong, K. (2000). *The Battle for God: Fundamentalism in Judaism, Christianity and Islam.* Hammersmith, London, HarperCollins Publishers.

Armstrong, K. (2005). *A Short History of Myth.* Edinburgh, Canongate.

Augustine "The City of God."

Barber, R. (1998). The human foreground. *Greek Civilisation: An introduction.* B. A. Sparkes. Oxford, Blackwell Publishers, Ltd.: 21 - 37.

Basford, K. (2004). *The Green Man.* Woodbridge, Boydell and Brewer.

Beard, M. and J. Henderson (1997). "With this body I thee worship: Sacred prostitution in antiquity." *Gender and History* **9**(3): 480 - 503.

Bennett, H. (1923). "The exposure of infants in ancient Rome." *The Classical Journal* **18**(6): 341 - 351.

Bennett, J. and V. Crowley (2001). *Magic and Mysteries of Ancient Egypt.* Newton Aboot, Godsfield Press, Ltd.

Boardman, J. (1997). *The Great God Pan: The survival of an image.* London, Thames and Hudson.

Borgeaud, P. (1988). *The Cult of Pan in Ancient Greece.* Chicago, University of Chicago Press.

Brock, R. (1994). "The labour of women in classical Athens." *The Classical Quarterly* **44**(2): 336 - 346.

Brown, E. L. (1977). "The Divine Name "Pan"." *Transactions of the American Philological Association* **107**: 57-61.

Brut-Zaidman, L. (1990). Pandora's daughters and rituals in Grecian cities. *A History of Women in the West: I. From ancient Goddesses to Christian saints.* P. Pantel.

Bullough (1993). *Women and Prostitution: A social history.* New York, Prometheus Books.

Burkert, W. (1985). *Greek Religion.* Oxford, Blackwell.

Callimachus *Hymn III, to Artemis.*

Cameron, A. (1932). "The exposure of children and Greek ethics." *The Classical Review* **46**(3): 105 - 114.

Campbell, J. (1949). *The Hero with a Thousand Faces.* Princeton, Princeton University Press.

Campbell, J. (2001). *Creative Mythology.* London, Souvenir Press (Educational and Academic) Ltd.

Carr, E. H. (1961). *What is History?* New York, Vintage Books.

Carroll, M. P. (1992). "Allomotifs and the psychoanalytic study of folk narratives: Another look at 'The roommate's death'." *Folklore* **103**(3): 225 - 234.

Cicero *De Natura Deorum.*

Clauss, J. J. (2003). "Once upon a Time on Cos: A Banquet with Pan on the Side in Theocritus "Idyll 7"." *Harvard Studies in Classical Philology* **101**.

Cleage, P. (1993). *Deals with the Devil.* New York, Ballantine Books.

Codellas, P. S. (1945). "Modern Greek Folklore: The Smerdaki." *The Journal of American Folklore* **58**(229): 236 - 244.

Cohen, D. (1989). "Seclusion, separation, and the status of women in Classical Athens." *Greece and Rome 2nd Series* **36**(1): 3 - 15.

Crowley, A. (1919). "Hymn to Pan." *The Equinox* **III**(1).

Daly, M. (1973). *Beyond God The Father:Toward a Philosophy of Women's Liberation*. Boston, Beacon Press.

David, J. (2000). "The exclusion of women in the Mithraic Mysteries: Ancient or modern?" *Numen* **47**(2): 121 - 141.

David, R. (2002). *Religion and Magic in Ancient Egypt*. London, Penguin Books.

Davidson, G. (1967). *A Dictionary of Angels: including the fallen angels*. New York, The Free Press.

Demosthenes *Against Neaera*.

Demosthenes. (1949). "Demosthenes with an English translation." Retrieved 6.01.08, from http://www.perseus.tufts.edu/cgi-bin/ptext?lookup=Dem.+59+122.

Diotima. (2004). "Dancing God." from http://www.shadowplayzine.com/20yr-Diotima-Dancing%20God.htm.

Diotima (2004). "Discord can be good for you." *Rational Paganism*.

Diotima (2004). "Thoughts on belief." *GreenMantle* **Samhain**.

Diotima (2005). Dancing God. *Refuge: Tales of Myth and Magick*. D. J. Lawrence, Konton: 2001.

Diotima (2005). Lament at Banias. *Refuge: Tales of Myth and Magick*. D. J. Lawrence, Konton: 15 - 18.

Diotima (2005). The Mirror. *Refuge: Tales of Myth and Magick*. D. J. Lawrence, Konton: 1 - 7.

Diotima (2005). *Refuge: Tales of myth and magick*, Konton Publishing.

Diotima (2005). "What makes a God?" *GreenMantle* **Spring**: 10 - 11.

Diotima (2006). Belief and knowledge. *Banish with Laughter: Essays on myth and magick*. D. J. Lawrence, Konton Press.

Diotima (2006). "By heart." *Pagan Dawn* **Beltaine**.

Diotima (2006). Christmas Card Deception. *Banish with Laughter*. D. J. Lawrence, Konton Press.

Duby, G. and M. Perrot (1990). Writing the history of women. *A History of Women in the West: I. From ancient Goddesses to Christian saints*. E. Pantel.

Duby & Perrot (1992). *A History of Women in the West*. Cambridge Mass, Belknap Press.

Dunsany, L. (2003). *The Blessing of Pan*, Wildside Press.

Ehernberg (1989). *Women in Prehistory*. British Museum Publications.

Eliot (1993). *The Global Myths: Exploring primitive, pagan, sacred and scientific mythologies*. London, Penguin Books Ltd.

Estes, P. (1992). *Women Who Run with the Wolves: Myths and stories of the wild woman archetype*. New York, Ballantine Books.

Euripides "Hippolytus."

Euripides *Medea*.

Euripides. (1850). "Bacchae." The Tragedies of Euripides, translated by T. A. Buckley. Retrieved 7.6.06, from http://perseus.uchicago.edu/hopper/toc.jsp?doc=Perseus:text:1999.01.0092:card=945.

Euripides. (1891). "Rhesus." The Plays of Euripides, translated by E. P. Coleridge. Volume I. London. . . Retrieved 7.6.06, from http://perseus.uchicago.edu/hopper/toc.jsp?doc=Perseus:text:1999.01.0120:card=34.

Euripides. (1938). "Iphigenia in Tauris." The Complete Greek Drama, edited by Whitney J. Oates and Eugene O'Neill, Jr. in two volumes. 1, translated by Robert Potter. New York.. . Retrieved 7.6.06, from http://perseus.uchicago.edu/hopper/toc.jsp?doc=Perseus:text:1999.01.0112:card=1123.

Faraone, C. (2004). "Ancient Greek Curse Tablets ", from http://fathom.lib.uchicago.edu/1/777777122300/.

Fletcher, J. (2003). *The Egyptian Book of Living and Dying*. London, Duncan Baird Publishers.

Frankfurter, D. (1995). "Roy Kotansky, Greek Magical Amulets: The Inscribed Gold, Silver, Copper, and Bronze Lamellae. Part I: Published Texts of Known Provenance. Papyrologica Coloniensia 22/1. Opladen: Westdeutscher Verlag, 1994 (Review)." *Bryn Mawr Classical Review* 4(12).

French, M. (1985). *Beyond power: On women, men and morals*. New York, Summit Books.

Gaiman, N. (2005). *American Gods*. London, Headline Review.

Garland, R. (1994). *Religion and the Greeks*. London, Bristol Classical Press.

Geddes and Grosset (1997). *Ancient Egypt Myth & Mystery*.

Georgoudi, S. (1990). Creating a myth of matriarchy. *A History of Women in the West: I. From ancient Goddesses to Christian saints*. P. Pantel.

Gordon, R. (1999). Imagining Greek and Roman Magic. *Witchcraft and Magic in Europe: Ancient Greece and Rome*. V. Flint, R. Gordon, G. Luck and D. Ogden. London, The Athlone Press.: 159 - 276.

Gould, J. (1980). "Law, Custom and Myth: Aspects of the social position of women in classical Athens." *The Journal of Hellenic Studies* **100**: 38 - 59.

Grahame, K. (1917). "The wind in the willows." Retrieved 7.5.06, from http://etext.virginia.edu/toc/modeng/public/GraWind.html.

Green (1992). *Dictionary of Celtic Myth and Legend*. London, Thames and Hudson Ltd.

Green, M. (2004). *The Gods of the Celts*. Thrupp, Sutton Publishing Ltd.

Griffiths, J. G. (1955). "The orders of the Gods in Greece and Egypt (According to Herodotus)." *The Journal of Hellenic Studies* **75**: 21 - 23.

Grimal, P. (1996). *The Dictionary of Classical Mythology* Oxford, Blackwell Publishing.

Haldane, J. A. (1968). "Pindar and Pan: frs. 95 - 100 Snell." *Phoenix* **22**(1): 18 - 31.

Hammond, N. G. L. (1968). "The Campaign and the Battle of Marathon." *The Journal of Hellenic Studies* **88**: 13-57.

Harrison, E. (1926). "PAN, PANEION, PANIKON." *The Classical Review* **40**(1): 6 - 8.

Herodotus (1972). *The Histories*. London, Penguin Books.

Hesiod (1999). *Theogony*. Oxford, Oxford Paperbacks.

Hillman, J. and W. Roscher (1972). *Pan and the Nightmare : Two Essays*. Woodstock, CT, Spring.

Holland, C. A. (1998). "After Antigone: Women, the past and the future of feminist political thought." *American Journal of Political Science* **42**(4): 1108 - 1132.

Homer (2003). *The Odyssey*. London, Penguin Books, Ltd.

Hyginus "Astronomica."

Hyginus *Fabulae*

Ingalls, W. (2002). "Demography and Dowries: Perspectives on female infanticide in classical Greece." *Phoenix* **56**(3/4): 246 - 254.

Inkubus Sukkubus. "Lord Of The Flame Lyrics." Retrieved 20.11.06, from http://www.lyricsdomain.com/9/inkubus_sukkubus/ lord_of_the_flame.html.

Johns, C. (1989). *Sex or Symbol: Erotic images of Greece and Rome.* London, The British Museum Press.

Johnstone, S. (2003). "Women, Property, and Surveillance in Classical Athens." *Classical Antiquity* 22(2): 247-274.

Katz, M. (1992). "Ideology and "The status of women" in ancient Greece." *History and Theory* 31(4): 70 - 97.

Keller, A. G. (1910). "The study of Homeric religion." *The American Journal of Sociology* 15(5): 641 - 656.

Keuls (1985). *The Reign of the Phallus.* Berkeley, University of California Press.

Kirk (1970). *Myth: Its meaning and function and in ancient and other cultures.* London, Cambridge University Press.

Kleinberg (1988). *Retrieving Women's History.* Berg Publishers.

Laquer, T. (1992). *Making Sex: Body and gender from the Greeks to Freud.* Cambridge, Mass., Harvard University Press.

Larson, J. (1997). "Handmaidens of Artemis?" *The Classical Journal* 92(3): 249 - 257.

Larson, J. (2001). *Greek Nymphs: Myth, cult, lore.* Oxford, Oxford University Press.

Lefkowitz (1986). *Women in Greek Myth.* London, Bristol Classical Press.

Lefkowitz and Fant (1992). *Women's Life in Greece and Rome: a source book in translation.* London, Gerald Duckworth and Co.

Longus (2002). *The Pastorals, or the Loves of Daphnis and Chloe.* Cambridge, Ontario, In parentheses Publications.

Lonsdale, S. H. (1993). *Dance and Ritual Play in Greek Religion.* Longon, The Johns Hopkins University Press.

Loraux, N. (1990). What is a Goddess? *A History of Women in the West: I. From ancient Goddesses to Christian saints.* P. Pantel. 1.

Lucian (1905). The double indictment. *The Works of Lucian of Samosata.* Oxford, The Clarendon Press.

Luck, G. (1999). Witches and sorcerers in classical literature. *Witchcraft and Magic in Europe: Ancient Greece and Rome.* V. Flint, R. Gordon, G. Luck and D. Ogden. London, The Athlone Press. 2: 91 - 158.

Lyons, D. (2003). "Dangerous Gifts: Ideologies of Marriage and Exchange in Ancient Greece." *Classical Antiquity* **22**(1): 93-134.

Machen, A. (1894). "The Great God Pan." Retrieved 29.5.06, from http://www.gutenberg.org/dirs/etext96/ggpan10.txt.

Mackail, J. W. "Select Epigrams from The Greek Anthology: Edited with a Revised Text, Translation, and Notes, by J. W. Mackail; London: Longmans, Green, and Co., 1890." Retrieved 5.8.06, from http://ancienthistory.about.com/od/greekanthology/a/GreekAnthology.htm.

Maranda, P., Ed. (1972). *Mythology*. Penguin Modern Sociology Readings. Harmondsworth, Penguin Books Limited.

Maurizio, L. (1995). "Anthropology and spirit possession: A reconsideration of the Pythia's role at Delphi." *The Journal of Hellenic Studies* **115**: 69 - 86.

McClure, L. K., Ed. *Sexuality and Gender in the Classical World: Readings and sources*. Interpreting Ancient History. Oxford, Blackwell Publishing.

Menander. (2006). "Dyskolos " Retrieved 24.12.07, 2007, from http://faculty.fairfield.edu/rosivach/cl103a/dyskolos.htm.

Merivale, P. (1969). *Pan the Goat-God*. Cambridge, MA, Harvard University Press.

Merivale, P. (1991). "The Cult of Pan in Ancient Greece." *The Journal of American Folklore* **104**(413): 390 - 382.

Metraux, G. P. R. (1999). "Ancient housing: "Oikos" and "Domus" in Greece and Rome." *The Journal of the Society of Architectural Historians* **58**(3): 392 - 405.

Moehring, H. R. (1959). "The persecution of the Jews and the adherents of the Isis cult at Rome in A.D. 19." *Novum Testamentum* **3**(4): 293 - 304.

Nagy, G. (1992). "Homeric Questions." *Transactions of the American Philological Association* **122**: 17 - 60.

Nonnus *Dionysiaca*.

Notopoulos, J. A. (1962). "The Homeric Hymns as oral poetry: A study of the Post-Homeric oral tradition." *The American Journal of Philology* **83**(4): 337 - 368.

O'Faolain, J. and L. Martines, Eds. (1973). *Not in God's Image: Women in History from the Greeks to the Victorians*. San Francisco CA, Harper & Row.

Ogden, D. (1999). Binding spells: Curse tablets and voodoo dolls in the Greek and Roman Worlds. *Witchcraft and Magic in Europe: Ancient Greece and Rome*. V. Flint, Gordon, R., Luck, G. and Ogden, D. London, The Athlone Press. 2.

Oppian *Halieutica*

Ovid *Fasti*.

Ovid (1955). *Metamorphoses*. London, Penguin.

Pantel, P. (1990). *A History of Women in the West: I. From ancient Goddesses to Christian saints*.

Patterson, C. (1985). ""Not worth the rearing": The causes of infant exposure in ancient Greece." *Transactions of the American Philological Association* **115**: 103 - 123.

Pausanias. "Description of Greece." Retrieved 3.6.06.

Pausanias *Guide to Greece*

Plato. (1921). "Cratylus." Plato in Twelve Volumes, Vol. 12; Harvard University Press, London, William Heinemann Ltd. translated by Harold N. Fowler. Cambridge, MA. Retrieved 21.7.06.

Polyaenus (1793). *Stratagems of War*. London, Ares Publishers, Inc.

Polybius *Histories*.

Porphyry *On Abstinence from Killing Animals*.

Pratchett, T. (1992). *Small Gods*. London, Corgi.

Pratt, L. H. (2000). "The Old Women of Ancient Greece and the Homeric Hymn to Demeter." *Transactions of the American Philological Association* **130** (0): 41 - 65.

Price, S. and E. Kearns, Eds. (2004). *The Oxford Dictionary of Classical Myth and Religion* Oxford, Oxford University Press.

Propertius, S. "Elegies." Vincent Katz, Ed. Retrieved 12/6/06, from http://perseus.uchicago.edu/hopper/toc.jsp?doc=Perseus:text: 1999.02.0067:book=1:poem=18.

Richardson, N. I. (2003). *The Homeric Hymns*. London, Penguin Classics.

Robbins, T. (2001). *Jitterbug Perfume*. Didsbury, No Exit Press.

Rousselle (1990). Body Politics in Ancient Rome. *A History of Women in the West: I. From ancient Goddesses to Christian saints*. Pantel.

Roy, J. (1999). "'Polis' and 'oikos' in classical Athens." *Greece and Rome 2nd Series* **46**(1): 1 - 18.

Schaps, D. M. (1989). "What was free about a free Athenian woman?" *Transactions of the American Philological Association* **128**: 161- 188.

Scheid (1990). The religious roles of Roman women. *A History of Women in the West: I. From ancient Goddesses to Christian saints*. Pantel.

Segal, R. A. (2004). *Myth: A very short introduction*. Oxford, Oxford University Press.

Shorter, E. (1983). *A History of Women's Bodies*, Allen Lane.

Sissa, G. (1990). The sexual philosophies of Plato and Aristotle. *A History of Women in the West: I. From ancient Goddesses to Christian saints*. P. Pantel.

Solanis, V. "S.C.U.M. Manifesto." Retrieved 11.1.07, from http://www.womynkind.org/scum.htm.

Sophocles *Ajax*.

Speake, G., Ed. (1994). *The Penguin Dictionary of Ancient History*. London, Penguin Books Ltd.

Statius *Thebaid*

Stillwell, R., W. L. MacDonald, et al. (1976). "The Princeton encyclopedia of classical sites." Princeton University Press. Retrieved 25.6.06, from http://perseus.uchicago.edu/hopper/toc.jsp?doc=Perseus:text: 1999.04.0006:entry=hymettos.

Strenski, I. (1987). *Four Theories of Myth in the 20th Century: Cassirer, Eliade, Levi-Strauss and Malinowski*. Basingstoke, The MacMillan Press.

Stroszeck, J. (2002). *Divine Protection for Shepherd and Sheep: Apollon, Hermes, Pan and their Christian counterparts St. Mamas, St. Themistocles and St. Modestos*. PECUS. Man and animal in antiquity., Swedish Institute in Rome.

Suidas "Panikoi deimati."

Sykes, E. and A. Kendall (2002). *Who's Who in Non-Classical Mythology*. London, Routledge.

Thomas, Y. (1990). The division of the sexes in Roman law. *A History of Women in the West: I. From ancient Goddesses to Christian saints*. P. Pantel.

Thornton, B. S. (1997). *Eros: The Myth of Ancient Greek Sexuality*. Boulder, Colorado, Westview Press.

Valerius Flaccus *Argonautica*.

Virgil *Georgics*.

Voss, B. L. (2000). "Feminisms, queer theories, and the archaeological study of past sexualities." *World Archaeology* **32**(2): 180–192.

Waterson, B. (1996). *The Gods of ancient Egypt*.

Wilson, J. F. (2004). *Caesarea Philippi : Banias, the lost city of Pan*. London.

Zaidman (1990). Pandora's Daughters and Rituals in Grecian Cities. *A History of Women in the West*. **1**.

About the Author

Diotima was the teacher who led Socrates to an appreciation of the nature of love and its relation to philosophy and the world in general. The current author is not Diotima of Mantinea, but she does believe firmly that the dichotomy between thought and feeling, between "mind" and "heart," has crippled Western society for far too long; she works in whatever way she can to redress that.

Diotima is, among other things, a mother, a lover, an inhabitant of bookshops, a teacher, a reader, a worker... (and much less energetic than this makes her sound!).

About the Bibliotheca Alexandrina

Ptolemy Soter, the first Makedonian ruler of Egypt, established the library at Alexandria to collect all of the world's learning in a single place. His scholars compiled definitive editions of the Classics, translated important foreign texts into Greek, and made monumental strides in science, mathematics, philosophy and literature. By some accounts over a million scrolls were housed in the famed library, and though it has long since perished due to the ravages of war, fire, and human ignorance, the image of this great institution has remained as a powerful inspiration down through the centuries.

To help promote the revival of traditional polytheistic religions we are launching a series of books dedicated to the ancient gods of Greece and Egypt. The library will be a collaborative effort drawing on the combined resources of the different elements within the modern Hellenic and Kemetic communities, in the hope that we can come together to praise our gods and share our diverse understandings, experiences and approaches to the divine.

For more information, please visit us at www.neosalexandria.org

Sincerely,

The Editorial Board of the Library of Neos Alexandria